CONTENTS

D0319448

WELCOME TO YOUR BODY!

This is a book about the body. It's about everybody's body and anybody's body – and it's about *your* body. It's about what's inside you, how it works and how it changes during your life.

You notice your body's aches and pains, its gurgles and its rumbles. Everything it does affects your life. Everything that happens to it changes your life. But scratch the surface and your body is more than interesting – it's amazing. It's so amazing – it's BRAIN-BOGGLING. *Horribly* brain-boggling!

OK – so it doesn't have super powers like X-ray vision or death-ray fingers. But who needs that stuff? Your body's brain-boggling secrets are far more exciting and far more surprising. To prove it we've called in a trio of tiny science experts. Say "Hi!" to the shrinking scientists …

THE BRAIN-BOGGLING BODY

starring THE SHRINKING SCIENTISTS...

Professor Small

Dr Sensible

Junior

I'M SENSIBLE...

...AND I'M NOT!

I MIGHT BE SMALL BUT I HAVE A GIANT INTELLECT!

Mr Fluffy is the scientists' pet rabbit. He's a brainy bunny...

Mr Fluffy

The shrinking scientists are going to explore the insides of this perfectly Normal Family.

Of course it's going to be Horrible Science. Of course it's going to be gruesome and gory. But that's the body – you can't get away from it. And who would want to? After all, where would you be without your body?

BORN TO BE ALIVE

The first brain-boggling fact about your body is that you're alive! Being alive is a wonderful feeling. After all, most things in the universe aren't alive – if you don't believe me ask a rock. And being alive is much more fun than being dead. Who wants to be a zombie anyway?

Mind you, being alive is complicated – as the shrinking scientists are about to find out. They're at the Normal House scanning the boy for signs of life …

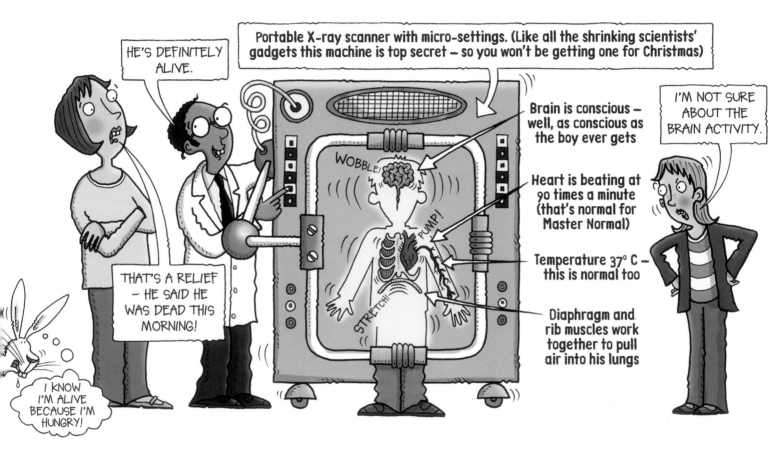

The most marvellous sign of life is being conscious. That means your brain knows who you are. (It would be embarrassing if you thought you were someone else.) And being conscious means your brain is busy putting together a picture of your surroundings that draws on your memories and allows you to play a part in the world around you. As I said, being alive is complicated – but so are you!

CRUCIAL CELLS

Your body needs to be the right temperature because its crucial chemistry only works within a narrow temperature range. And most of it happens in your cells.

"So what's a cell?" I hear you mutter. Well, it's nothing to do with prison cells, cell phones or cellos. Cells are boffin-speak for your brain-boggling body-building blocks. The shrinking scientists are studying a cell from the boy's dandruff … it's a sickening sight.

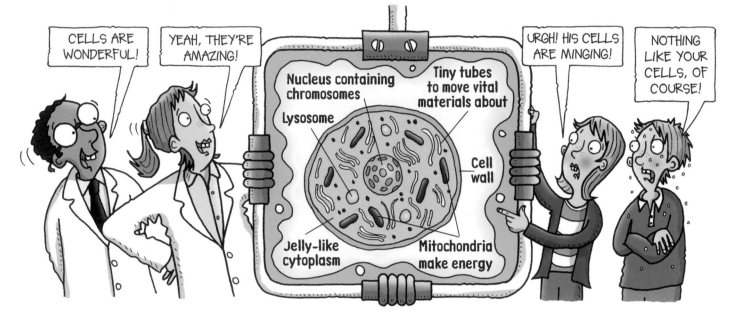

Each of your cells is like a tiny city. There's a wall to keep out intruders, a transport network and a library. The library is the nucleus containing your chromosomes. Your chromosomes are like books of genes – the chemical codes to build a whole new body – but unlike ordinary books they can copy themselves and give orders.

There are even power stations and rubbish carts. The power stations are called mitochondria – they turn a type of sugar called glucose into energy. The rubbish carts are bags of digestive juice called lysosomes that guzzle up worn-out bits of cell.

Instead of people, your cell city contains millions of protein molecules* – imagine them as robots controlled by the chromosomes. Your breathtaking body contains about 50 million million micro-marvel cells. Every minute 300 million of them get destroyed and replaced by other cells dividing.

*Molecules = groups of atoms bonded together. Protein = a type of molecule made of chains of smaller molecules called amino acids.

Although proteins sound brain-splattingly complicated, like the rest of you they're made of simple ingredients. Just imagine you could grow a human in a flowerpot – what would it be made from?

The carbon inside you is the same stuff that forms coal, and it's great for building body molecules. The hydrogen is lighter than air – if you were completely made of this stuff you'd float to the ceiling and blow up if you went near a candle. Your bones and teeth are mainly phosphorus and calcium. Phosphorus glows in the dark, and calcium is also found in chalk and marble tombstones. All this chemistry means that your brain-boggling body is a busy place …

YOUR BUSY BODY

AN "H"!

At this second your body is reading. The retinas (light-detecting areas) at the back of your eyeballs are picking up images of the letters on this page and sending them to your brain through your optic nerves. In a split second your brain recognizes the funny black squiggles and tells you what they mean

Your stomach is cheerfully squelching your food every 20 seconds. In your guts, some of this food is being parcelled into balls and squished along the long rubbery-velvety tube at a speed of 2.8 cm per minute

UH?

Meanwhile, all over your body, millions of cells are processing glucose and protein from your blood and using glucose and oxygen to make energy

Some cells are dividing

PLIP! PLIP! PLIP!

and others are quietly destroying themselves. Your cells digest themselves at the end of their lives

SQUEEEEEZE!

At present you're fairly relaxed, but even so some of your muscles are working hard to hold your back up and grip the cover of this book. The muscles are squeezing and tugging on the bones of your hands and in your backbone

Deep inside your body, your kidneys are busy filtering waste chemicals and spare water from your blood and sending them down the tube to your bladder. Here, stretch receptors are politely telling your brain that you'll soon need the loo

YOU NEED A WEE!

LUB-DUB! LUB-DUB!

Also at this moment your blood is being propelled round your body by your heart. More blood is surging into your lungs as they puff out

SO YOU SEE, EVEN WHEN YOU'RE DOING NOTHING MUCH YOUR BODY IS DOING A LOT.

At the Normal's, the boy wants to know what his body is up to – so the scientists have wired him up to a loudspeaker…

It's the end of the day. The family are off to bed but it's going to be a long night for the scientists. They're staying up to study the family's sleeping habits.

SCARY SLEEP

Your brain is only two per cent of your body's weight but it has 100 per cent of your personality, dreams and imagination. It's also the body bit that makes you sleep and dream, and right now the other shrinking scientists are trying to figure out the strange secrets of Junior's brain…

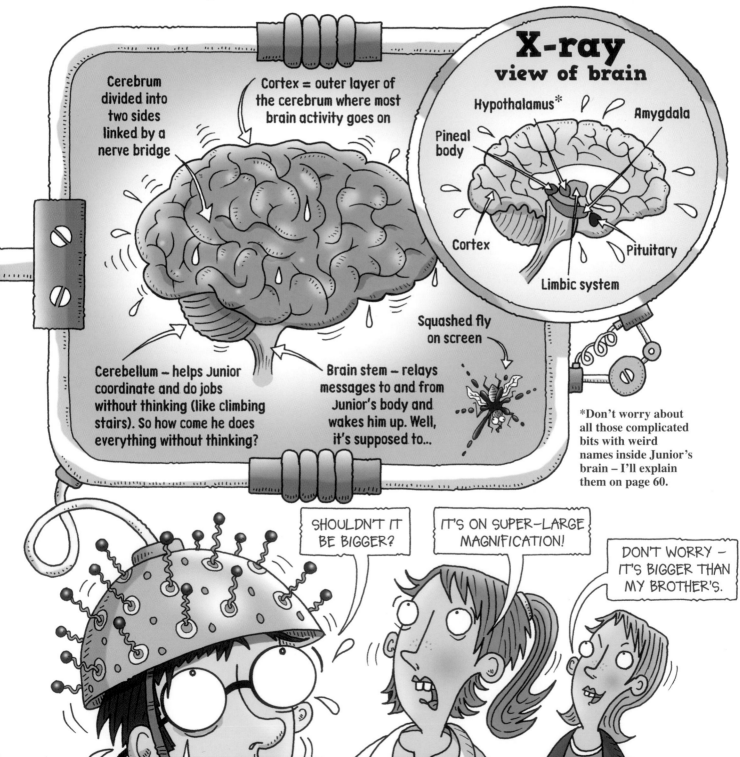

Cerebrum divided into two sides linked by a nerve bridge

Cortex = outer layer of the cerebrum where most brain activity goes on

X-ray view of brain

Hypothalamus*

Amygdala

Pineal body

Cortex

Pituitary

Limbic system

Cerebellum – helps Junior coordinate and do jobs without thinking (like climbing stairs). So how come he does everything without thinking?

Brain stem – relays messages to and from Junior's body and wakes him up. Well, it's supposed to...

Squashed fly on screen

*Don't worry about all those complicated bits with weird names inside Junior's brain – I'll explain them on page 60.

SHOULDN'T IT BE BIGGER?

IT'S ON SUPER-LARGE MAGNIFICATION!

DON'T WORRY – IT'S BIGGER THAN MY BROTHER'S.

At the Normal house it's midnight and the sleeping family are wired-up to EEG* machines that monitor their brainwaves. The shrinking scientists are making notes.

Notes on the Normal family's sleeping habits
By the shrinking scientists

12 am: The zonked-out family are drifting through the deeper stages of sleep.

12.45 am: They're asleep less deeply and now they're dreaming. This is called REM (rapid-eye-movement) sleep. Looks like Mr Fluffy's dreaming too.

2.30 am: Yawn! We could do with more black coffee. The family are deeply asleep again – I wish we were. Wake up, Junior!

6 am: The family have had two more periods of dreaming and two more periods of deep sleep – but not as deep as before. They dream for longer each time.

7 am: They've woken up feeling refreshed and ready for the day. Unlike us zzzzzz...

Dreaming is like a crazy cinema stuck between your ears. But boffins don't think you dream for fun. They reckon that dreaming helps you to remember what you learn. (Try this excuse when you get caught kipping in class.) Dreaming might also suggest answers to life's little problems. Hmm – if you get caught kipping in class it's more likely to *cause* problems!

Mind you, that doesn't stop dreams from being weird. Dreaming doesn't involve the cortex – the brain bit you reason with. And that means when you see something silly you don't think "Whoa – that's impossible!" – you just accept it.

*EEG = electroencephalograph (e-leck-tro-en-ce-fa-la-graf). These are real machines that draw lines showing electrical activity in the brain.

WAKE UP, SLEEPY-HEAD!

All this sleep info raises a brain-boggling question. It's the sort of brain-boggler that might keep you awake at night – if you were a scientist. The question is, why sleep at all? I mean, what's the point of boring old shut-eye when there are so many more exciting things to do?

Well, for one thing it doesn't matter how determined you are to stay awake, your body is even more determined to make you sleep. Here's how. In your hypothalamus is a tiny blob of cells that connects with the nerves linking your eyeballs with the vision centre at the back of your brain. This blob detects how much light you see, and when your brain senses that it's night, your pineal body dishes out a substance called melatonin to make you sleepy.

And maybe that's a blessing in disguise because look what happens when you don't get enough sleep…

Junior the next day…

And there's another thing. If you're still up at three in the morning you feel terrible. Scientists have found that people awake at this time feel colder because their body temperature has dropped by six per cent. They're useless at maths (well, some people are during the day) and, to make things worse, they're more likely to have an accident. So I guess snoring your head off is better than getting it knocked off.

Sleepy-head QUIZ

Here's a quiz simple enough to do in your sleep.

TRUE or FALSE?

GROAN!

ZZZZZ

1 Lack of sleep causes bags under your eyes.

2 Your grandparents need more sleep than a baby.

3 People with round heads are less likely to snore.

COOL!

4 You can sleep with your eyes open.

ZZZz

DRIBBLE!

Answers:

1 FALSE. Dark circles in fair skin are caused by the dark blood showing through the thin skin under the eyes. This could be a sign of ill heath linked to lack of sleep. Oh all right, you can have half a point for true.

2 FALSE. New-born babies sleep around 16 hours a day (but not all at once). Your grandparents probably get by with six hours. They dream less than you but spend more time dozing.

3 FALSE. According to US scientists in 2002 they're MORE likely to snore because of the shape of their airways.

4 TRUE. When you're dreaming you can't move because your spinal cord doesn't relay messages from your brain. But if you sleep with your eyes open you can see the ghosts and monsters from your dreams in your own bedroom and you can't move a muscle!

VITAL VISION

It's eye-opening what your eyes can do. The scientists find this out as they scan one of Mrs Normal's squishy eyeballs.

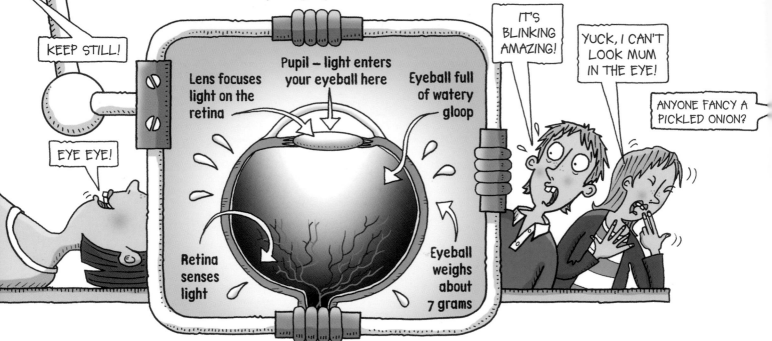

KEEP STILL!

EYE EYE!

Lens focuses light on the retina

Pupil – light enters your eyeball here

Eyeball full of watery gloop

IT'S BLINKING AMAZING!

YUCK, I CAN'T LOOK MUM IN THE EYE!

ANYONE FANCY A PICKLED ONION?

Retina senses light

Eyeball weighs about 7 grams

The secret of seeing is your light-sensing cells. In each retina you've got 4.5 million cone cells for viewing colours and 90 million rod cells. The rod cells can sense 10 million shades of grey and spot a candle flame 80 km away.

And here's how these splendid sensors work. Make a fist with one hand and wrap your other hand around it. You've made the shape of a molecule called "visual purple" that's found in your retina. Visual purple consists of two smaller molecules but when the light shines on it, one opens out and visual purple falls apart. It's just like you opening the hand around your fist. This releases energy that zaps nerve signals to your brain.

1 SQUEEZE!

2 HEY, BRAIN...

...TAKE A LOOK AT THIS!

Visual purple even helps you see in the dark. At first you can't see much because you need a lot of visual purple to detect the small amount of light there is. And it takes a while for your retinas to make enough vital visual purple for the job.

Another reflex makes you blink your eyes in bright light. It protects your sensitive retinas from being blinded by the light and gives your eyeballs an automatic wash. This saves you the bother – I mean, when was the last time you had to wash your eyeballs?

Can you read these facts without blinking?

1 You blink less if you're happy or reading. Or even when you're happily reading this book.

2 Children blink less than adults and everyone blinks more than cats. They only blink twice a minute and that's why cats can give you an unnerving stare. Now that's a blinking liberty.

WHAT ARE YOU STARING AT?

3 Each of your eyelids weighs 0.57 grams – that's the same as a hummingbird's tongue.

I bet you never noticed this – but every time you blink, your upper eyelid twists slightly and rolls debris off your eyeball towards the pink triangle at the corner of your eye. Here there's a tunnel to the snotty corridors behind your nose. Any germs or dirt on your eyeball end up stuck in the snot and you eventually gulp it down with your breakfast. Some of your tears end up here too, and that's why people get a snotty nose when they cry.

URGH!

PLOP!

A GOOD SCRUB DOWN

You might think that you own your body. If so your brain might be boggled to read that billions of bacteria* think you're a luxury liner. And right now they're enjoying free central heating and gourmet germ dinners with their festering friends ...

At this moment about 80 varieties of bacteria are slithering between your teeth and greedily gobbling what's left of your last meal. Meanwhile, 10 million tiny terrors are frolicking on every square centimetre of your skin. And if that sounds 10 million too many, you won't want to read that greasy skin (such as your forehead or the sides of your nose) has ten times more bacteria. And right now they're cheerfully slurping up your delicious skin oils.

Over in the Normal house an argument has broken out...

I BET YOU'VE GOT BILLIONS OF BACTERIA!

NOT AS MANY AS YOU!

The shrinking scientists are about to take a close look at the boy's bacteria. The brave boffins stand under their top-secret shrinking ray and soon they're a microscopic size.

*Bacteria are microbes consisting of one cell but no proper nucleus.

18

Look at that lovely mite! Everyone on Earth, including you and me, has these curious creatures snuggling at the base of their eyelashes. They climb aboard when you touch foreheads or share towels with someone else. Mites are harmless but they're horribly interesting, as we found out when we interviewed one…

Still, let's be positive – with your friendly crew of eyelash mites you'll always have someone to talk to, and they do guzzle those beastly bacteria.

DISGUSTING DUST

Are you gagging at those beastly body bacteria? If you're running around screaming – STOP IT RIGHT NOW! You'll give the cat a heart attack and in any case there's no point. You can't get rid of bacteria. Oh well, most of them are harmless – or 'armless anyway. And what's more they're doing you a favour. By taking up skin space they stop more harmful bugs from moving in.

And your body has a clever way to get rid of unwanted guests. You shed your skin. During your life, you'll shed about 47.6 kg of skin – that's equal to 1,000 layers of birthday suit – and every falling flaky fragment takes hundreds of bacteria with it.

Bet you never knew!
New Zealand artist Dane Mitchell grew germs from skin flakes to create a work of art. Mind you, that's not too strange – in 2004, Uruguayan artist Carlos Capelan made his toenail clippings into artwork. Would you make an exhibition of yourself?

So where does all your skin go (assuming you're not saving it for your art homework)? Well, you might see skin flakes dancing in a sunbeam or come across them lurking in a pair of pants that you've been wearing for a month – but most end up scattered around your home. You call it "dust".

Now back to their usual size, the shrinking scientists are using their specially invented micro-thermal scanner to track the family's skin flakes … much to Mrs Normal's annoyance.

Warmth makes dust rise at the centre of the room

Cooler walls make dust sink at the edges

OI! I'M TRYING TO WATCH TELLY!

I COULD HAVE SWORN I DUSTED THERE YESTERDAY...

IT'S EATEN BY MICROSCOPIC MITES RELATED TO YOUR EYELASH PAL.

COOL!

THERE'S A HUGE SKIN FLAKE HERE!

GROSS!

THAT'S A CORNFLAKE, JUNIOR!

Dust settles on shelves

Or under the sofa

Dust wafted about by the family's movements

But, there's more to dust than dead skin and bacteria. There might be tiny bits of dirt brought in from the outside, and if you're very lucky you might find some crusty dried earwax. Like your skin, earwax is a defence against germs, and scientists have actually found out what it's made of…

Body cookbook

Here's lovely crunchy homemade earwax – delicious with toast!

Ingredients:

Cerumen (oily-milky stuff produced in the outer part of your earhole)

Dried skin cells

Bits of hair

Dead bacteria and fungi

Method:

Mix all the ingredients and leave in a warm earhole for a few weeks until dry and crusty. The earwax should then drop out.

VOOSH! SPLURP! SPLOOP!

Cerumen stops your earhole getting dry and sore and it traps dirt, germs and fungi. That lovely crispy light-brown colour darkens in the air – so it's best to store your earwax in an airtight jar if you want to share it with your friends.

HMMM, IT LOOKS LIKE PEANUT BUTTER…

Toast

YEAH, CRUNCHY PEANUT BUTTER!

HORRIBLE HAIR

Along with dead skin, bacteria, dirt and earwax, the shrinking scientists have found plenty of hairs. Your hair is dead and made of a protein called keratin. There's more keratin in your nails, bird feathers and rhino horns too.

Each of your hairs is coated with waterproof gunk called sebum and squeezed from a tiny pit in your scalp at the speed of 1 cm per month. Meanwhile at the Normal's the scientists are off to take a horribly close look at the girl's hair…

Scientists aren't sure why your body isn't completely hairy. After all being hairy works fine for chimps – so why doesn't your brother look like one?

Well, lots of hair would keep us warm and provide protection against sunburn, but it also takes ages to clean and provides a great home for bloodsucking bugs. Your bare skin is easier to clean and it allows you to sweat to cool down. (Just think of what sweat does to your hair and you'll agree that sweaty and hairy isn't good news.) It's a brain-boggling fact that your body actually has as many hairs as chimps (yes it DOES), but most of our hairs are so small that you can't easily see them.

Sweat is constantly oozing from your body. It seeps from glands (a posh name for body-juice-making bits) in your skin. It's mostly water and its job is to take heat from your body as it dries into the air.

Over in the Normal house, all this talk about bacteria has persuaded Mr Normal to take a shower. But he reckons without the shrinking scientists… The boffins have shrunk down to check if he's washing properly… And he's NOT!

A BIT OF A MOUTHFUL

There's more to eating than munching and burping. Eating is about feeding your body with energy. This energy gets you up in the morning and keeps you alive. Scientists call this stomach-churning process "digestion".

The shrinking scientists are inspecting some of the quarter of a tonne of food the Normal family gobbles every year. The family aren't too happy. They're ready for their lunch … and Mr Fluffy is positively dribbling with hunger!

There's a nice mixture of different foods.

Your body breaks carbohydrate and sugar molecules down into glucose to feed your cells

Your body can break down fat molecules and store them for those moments when you're hungry enough to chomp the cat

CHOMP!

Vitamin C is found in fresh fruit and vegetables – the body can't store it so you need to munch plenty of fresh fruit and salad

MUNCH!

The protein is handy for repairing and making cells

Most types of foods contain vitamins – they're vital substances that your body needs in small amounts to stay healthy

Roughage keeps the other food moving through your guts

Snotty sniffing

A big part of preparing your body for the all-important act of scoffing is the smell of your supper. If it happened to pong of cow poo or stale stink bombs you might not want to risk sinking your choppers into it. And that's part of your nose's job – to warn you when something isn't good to eat.

Every time you sniff your supper, food molecules waft up the snotty passages behind your nose. And buried in the slimy snot are two smell-sensitive patches of tiny hairs just waiting to pick up molecules. They send nerve signals to your brain. Scientists think you can identify 2,000 different whiffs, but not everyone can spot the same smells.

Side effect of too much cabbage

PARP!

Bet you never knew!
Chewing and bubble gums have hardly any food value – but we love them. In 1995 it was reported that Harriet Sky of Denver, USA, had been chewing the same piece of bubble gum for 33 years. And I bet she never shared it with anyone.

SLOBBERY SPIT

Here's a brain-boggling question. What's it like to be eaten? Well, you start off on the quivering, drooling tongue. Squirts of slippery spit bathe you in thick gooey dribble. The saliva makes you gooey and starts to dissolve you to release your lovely tastes and smells. And then the terrible teeth descend to chop you to bits.

Your tongue is possibly your most amazing muscle. I mean, what other muscle could toss a partly chewed carrot in one direction and a chunk of chewy chicken in the other whilst talking? And talking about talking tongues – here's a more interesting method to torture your teacher than telling terrible teacher jokes…

Teacher's tea-break teaser

Knock politely on the staffroom door. When it opens calmly stick out your tongue and ask…

HOT HOON ISH NY HUNGUE HACKACHED HOO?*

SPLUTTER!

*WHAT BONE IS MY TONGUE ATTACHED TO?

Answer: 99.9 per cent of teachers don't know the answer and they might get a bit tongue-tied or even bite their tongue. In fact there's a small bone under your tongue called the hyoid.

While we've been talking, your salivary glands have been pumping out more spit – each day they make 0.75 litres of delightfully gooey liquid. At the Normal's, the shrinking scientists are studying sickening samples of the family's drool…

JUST A THIMBLEFUL MORE…

SPIT IT OUT – I WANT MY LUNCH!

WHAT A DRIP!

Body cookbook

Here's a mouth-watering dribble drink – ideal for serving with every meal!

Ingredients:

Water

Mucus – this snotty stuff lines many passages of the body and contains a protein called mucin

Nice healthy dissolved minerals

Sodium bicarbonate

Germ-killing substances such as lysozyme

Dead cells from your mouth and tongue

Urea and uric acid – waste body products found in urine (that's wee to non-scientists)

Several million bacteria (the germ-killers don't kill them all)

Enzymes for digesting fat and carbohydrate (see page 32)

Method:

Mix all the ingredients in a warm mouth until your dribble drink is thick and frothy.

Warning – it's not polite to share your dribble drink with your guests at a dinner party. Your guests will be perfectly happy to make their own.

SPLOOP!

SPLURP!

DROOL!

The sodium bicarbonate is the same stuff your mum might use for cooking (but it's not made from spit). It's there because your mouth bacteria make tooth-dissolving acids. Your brilliant bi-carb blocks the awful acids and saves your pearly whites from getting worn away.

Sadly even the busiest brushing can't scrub off all the bacteria, but you'll be relieved to know that you also have larger slimy microbes called amoebae (a-mee-b-eye) that guzzle germs for you. If the bacteria get the upper hand they'll make the stomach-turning stink known as bad breath…

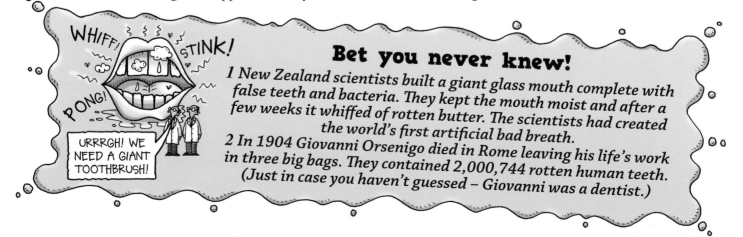

WHIFF!

STINK!

PONG!

URRRGH! WE NEED A GIANT TOOTHBRUSH!

Bet you never knew!

1 New Zealand scientists built a giant glass mouth complete with false teeth and bacteria. They kept the mouth moist and after a few weeks it whiffed of rotten butter. The scientists had created the world's first artificial bad breath.

2 In 1904 Giovanni Orsenigo died in Rome leaving his life's work in three big bags. They contained 2,000,744 rotten human teeth. (Just in case you haven't guessed – Giovanni was a dentist.)

TASTELESS TASTING

Your mouth is a busy place. While you're busily munching your lunch, your microbe mates are busily lunching on your leftovers and your tongue is busily tasting your meal.

The tiny bumps you can see on your tongue hide tiny taste buds. Here, sensor cells detect five flavours from food molecules in your spit. These are sweet, salt, bitter, sour and umami (a sort of savoury meaty taste). In fact, 80 per cent of what you think is taste is smell triggered by food molecules drifting up your nose from the back of your throat.

Dare you discover
how to fool your taste buds?
Phantom coffee

You will need:

Blindfold

Mug

Kettle

A jar of freshly roasted or freeze-dried coffee

Adult victim (er, sorry, volunteer)

NERVOUS SHAKE!

What you do:

1 Boil the water in the kettle and allow it to cool until it's not too hot to drink.

Take care BOILING WATER!

OOER!

2 Blindfold your volunteer.

3 Pretend to make them some coffee.

GLUG!

-TING!

SLURP!

4 Offer your victim a mug of hot water. Place the opened coffee jar close to their nose.

HMMM, DELICIOUS!

You should find:
They think they're drinking coffee because they can smell it.

Dare you discover
how to fool your taste buds?
Washed-out cheese

You will need:

Table knife
Parmesan cheese

STINKY PONG!

What you do:

1 Cut two small pieces of the cheese.

SPLOOOOOSH!

2 Wash one piece under a tap.

3 Taste the washed cheese and compare it to the unwashed piece.

LUVVERLEY!

RUBBERY!

You should find:

Yeoch! The washed cheese tastes flavourless and rubbery. Parmesan has crystals of a substance called monosodium glutamate (mo-no-so-dee-um glu-ta-mate) with an umami flavour on its surface. Wash the cheese and you wash away the taste. What a waste!

At last the scientists allow the family to eat. Like you, their appetite (desire for food) and even their sense of taste are affected by mood. (That's why people don't feel too hungry after an argument.) The place where you eat is also important – you might feel a bit less hungry if your dinner was served in the dog's bowl next to the toilet. Well my advice is to tuck in now. You won't feel too hungry after the next few pages…

Bet you never knew!

Some people keep their food in their mouths for ages and chew it 142 times – others gulp it down. In fact it doesn't matter too much as long as your grub is in bits small enough to swallow and is well-splattered with slimy spit.

TUCK IN? DON'T MIND IF I DO!

YOUR GURGLING GUTS

The shrinking scientists are keen to see digestion in action and the girl has volunteered to be scanned...

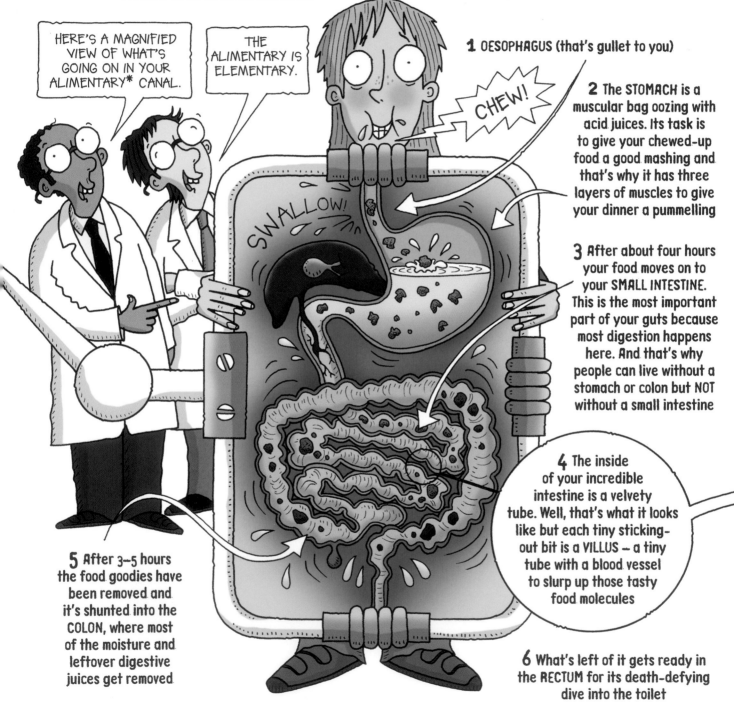

HERE'S A MAGNIFIED VIEW OF WHAT'S GOING ON IN YOUR ALIMENTARY* CANAL.

THE ALIMENTARY IS ELEMENTARY.

CHEW!

SWALLOW!

1 OESOPHAGUS (that's gullet to you)

2 The STOMACH is a muscular bag oozing with acid juices. Its task is to give your chewed-up food a good mashing and that's why it has three layers of muscles to give your dinner a pummelling

3 After about four hours your food moves on to your SMALL INTESTINE. This is the most important part of your guts because most digestion happens here. And that's why people can live without a stomach or colon but NOT without a small intestine

4 The inside of your incredible intestine is a velvety tube. Well, that's what it looks like but each tiny sticking-out bit is a VILLUS – a tiny tube with a blood vessel to slurp up those tasty food molecules

5 After 3–5 hours the food goodies have been removed and it's shunted into the COLON, where most of the moisture and leftover digestive juices get removed

6 What's left of it gets ready in the RECTUM for its death-defying dive into the toilet

*Posh science word for the guts.

30

Dreadful digestion details

Your stomach has a problem. In order to break up the food molecules and kill germs it contains dilute hydrochloric acid. This dissolves bacteria but it can dissolve you too. To save you from this unpleasant fate, your stomach is lined with slimy mucus. But its cells are always being digested. In the past minute ONE MILLION of your stomach cells have been turned into goo by your hungry stomach juices. Brain-boggling!

Mind you, if that sounds sickening you won't want to know what happens when digestion goes wonky. Let's imagine that loads of bacteria or their poisons (toxins) invade your guts. Your small intestine protests by sending what's left of your dinner back to your stomach. But your stomach doesn't want it and opens its valves at both ends. The half-digested food whizzes past the stomach and, helped by your strongly squeezing diaphragm muscle, up it comes with a generous squirt of stomach acid.

But not all of it. Your colon has a plan of its own. If it detects toxins or other nasties it goes into reverse and squirts water instead of sucking it up. Then it squeezes out the watery goo, and the revoltingly runny results get you running to the loo.

YOUR LOVELY LIVER

There's more to digestion than squeezing your supper through a tube. The brain-boggling bit happens in your slimy digestive juices. Here proteins called enzymes help to break up food molecules. Just imagine tiny mixing bowls where molecules can break up or mix and join. They speed digestion and keep your body fed – and that's just the start. Enzymes speed up all sorts of chemical changes that keep you alive.

Your cells can't use all the food from your meal at once. Instead your body stores the vital goodies. The body bit that sorts all this out is your liver. So it's no coincidence that your liver is the first port of call for the molecules from your dinner.

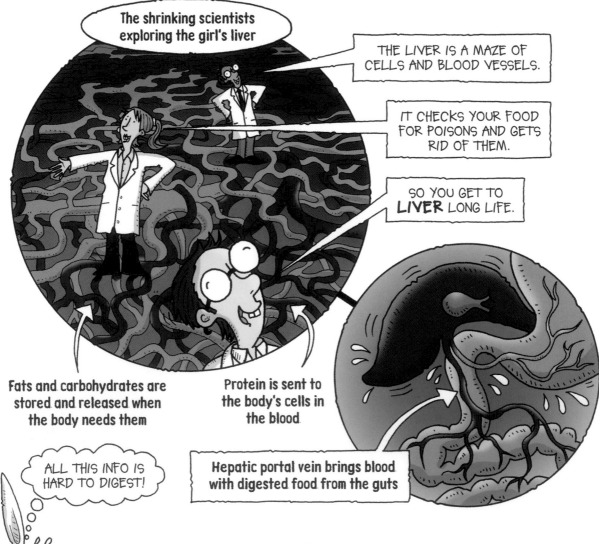

The shrinking scientists exploring the girl's liver

THE LIVER IS A MAZE OF CELLS AND BLOOD VESSELS.

IT CHECKS YOUR FOOD FOR POISONS AND GETS RID OF THEM.

SO YOU GET TO **LIVER** LONG LIFE.

Fats and carbohydrates are stored and released when the body needs them

Protein is sent to the body's cells in the blood.

Hepatic portal vein brings blood with digested food from the guts

ALL THIS INFO IS HARD TO DIGEST!

32

Thanks to your hard-working liver, your cells enjoy a tasty supper of hot blood-soup flavoured with glucose. And your mitochondria power stations can turn your food into super-charged energy to keep you alive. There's a lot of complicated chemistry going on, so the shrinking scientists have drawn us a handy diagram…

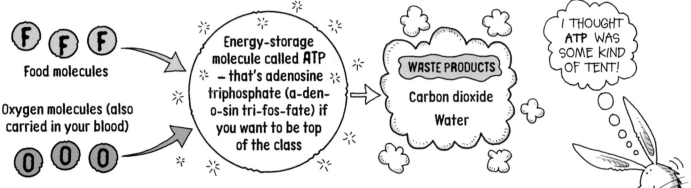

Whenever you need it your cells simply break apart the awesome ATP and release its stored power. The carbon dioxide wafts out in your breath and some of the water ends up in your sweat and pee and moisture in your breath.

Sorting the waste substances and spare water for your pee is the job of your kidneys. Your kidneys are a pair of fantastic filters that pass your blood through looping tubes to take back what your body needs. Together they sort out a litre of pee every day. And by some horrid coincidence, the shrinking scientists have just finished their lab analysis of the boy's pee…

IT'S BASICALLY 95 PER CENT WATER, TWO PER CENT UREA, ONE PER CENT SALT AND THE REST IS WASTE PRODUCTS SUCH AS URIC ACID AND AMMONIA SALT WITH A PINCH OF CALCIUM AND PHOSPHATE.

THAT LOOKS A WEE BIT HEAVY.

Bet you never knew!

Emperor Frederick II of Germany (1194–1250) enjoyed cruel experiments. In one test he gave two men a superb supper. One man was sent hunting and the other was sent to bed. In the morning both men had their guts cut open and fiendish Fred's doctor announced that the man who had slept had digested his dinner better. But he may have told Fred what he wanted to hear for fear of ending up as another of the Emperor's little experiments…

SOMETHING TO TALK ABOUT

You'll spend about ten years of your life talking. That's ten years *during* your life NOT ten years talking non-stop. If you tried to talk non-stop your teacher would give you a stern talking-to about why you shouldn't be talking.

It all began when you were about one year old. Human babies are interested in faces and familiar voices. They want to copy what adults say but all they can say is "goo-goo". Maybe you were trying to order your parents about, but your half-witted parents just burbled back. Then one day you spoke your first word and your excited parents told you how clever you were. And they've been telling you to be quiet ever since!

At 18 months you knew the grand total of 22 words. Six months later you could say another 250 words and by the time you were three you were busily learning a new word every hour. You ought to have been pleased with yourself – talking is a horribly hard skill to learn.

Over in the Normal house the scientists are studying how the boy talks.

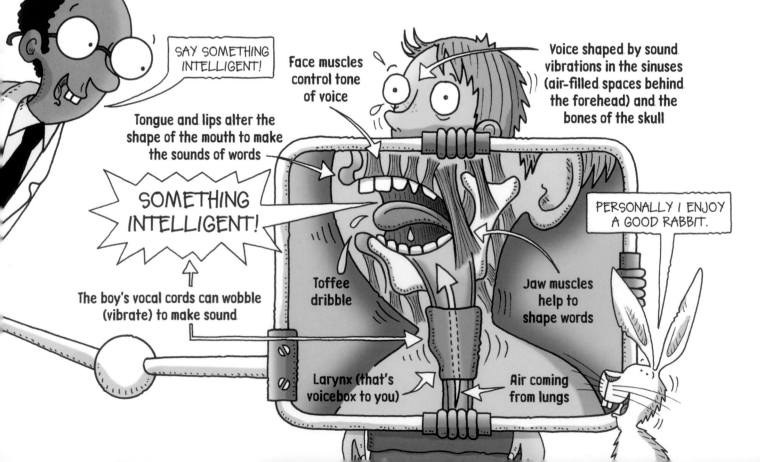

When it comes to talking – there's a lot to talk about. Let's start with your vital vocal cords. They're actually two fleshy folds at the top of your windpipe. They open when you breathe in – which is why you can't talk and breathe in – and they vibrate to make sounds. But even when you're enjoying a good natter, your vocal cords are silent half the time (tell that to your teacher next time they tell you off for chatting in class!).

Dare you discover
how important your vocal cords are?

You will need:

Yourself and your vocal cords

What you do:

1 Hold your breath and make sure you don't breathe out.
2 Say the word "the" as loudly as you can.
3 Try to say the word "thin" as loudly as you can.

You should find:

It's possible to say "the" because you don't actually need vocal cords to make the sound. It's harder to say "thin" because you need your vocal cords and they need breath from your lungs.

If you had no vocal cords you would find it hard to say anything – but what makes you sound like you is the way you alter noises from your vocal cords. Your tongue and lip movements and the shape of your throat, skull bones and sinuses play a part. And together they ensure that your voice is totally unique. No one on Earth – not even your brother or sister or pet parrot – sounds exactly like you.

Bet you never knew!
An Italian singing star gave permission for his larynx to be removed after his death. But when scientists blew air through the dead man's vocal cords all they got was a rude noise like blowing a raspberry.

THPLURRRRP!

To bring back his singing voice they needed the rest of his head.

HORRIBLE HEARING

How high or loud your voice sounds is called your 'tone of voice'. It really depends on the person you're talking to. You might bellow a cheery "HEEELLOOO ME OLD MUCKER!" to your friend but if you said that to your teacher bad things are sure to happen. That's why it's wise to tell your teacher about your missing homework in a quiet tone of voice.

"But how do I hear?" I hear you say…

1 Sounds take the form of vibrating air molecules that bump into other molecules to make sound waves like ripples on a pond.

2 The ear – scientists call the part you see the "pinna". The pinna catches sound waves and directs them into your ear canal (that's ear 'ole to you)

3 The eardrum is held tight by a muscle. It vibrates (wobbles) when sound waves hit it. The louder the sound the harder the eardrum vibrates, and the higher the sound the faster it vibrates

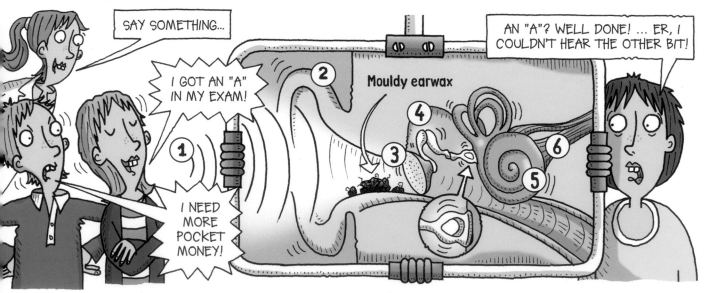

4 Bones in the middle ear pass on the sound and make it louder. The stapes bone passes on sound to the cochlea

5 The cochlea contains thousands of tiny fibres, each sensitive to vibes of a particular speed (scientists say "frequency")

6 Vibes are turned into nerve signals that go to the brain

You might wonder how your ear bones can turn up the volume. Well, your eardrum is about 10 mm across, and that's larger than the area whacked by the stapes. Squeezing the force of the vibe into a smaller area makes it stronger and louder. Now that's an idea worth shouting about!

Could you be a scientist?

You've got the brain-boggling ability to listen to one sound amongst many. This allows you to hear your friend at a noisy party or catch someone gossiping about you across the playground.

In the 1970s scientists tested this ability by training volunteers to expect a nasty electric shock whenever they heard a city name. Here's Junior to show us the next stage of the experiment...

Different words played through each ear

Volunteers had to repeat the words they heard through one ear whilst ignoring the words in their other ear

BANJO...
PUMPKIN...
POTTY...
RICE PUDDING...
AARDVARK...
SAUCEPAN...
LEECH...
PIMPLE...
WEASEL...
FRIED EGG...
FROGSPAWN...
FOX...

FOX? WHERE?

Sweat sensors on hand to detect fear

The dreaded city name was amongst the words the volunteers weren't supposed to be listening to. What happened next?

a) The volunteers felt strangely scared but didn't know why.

b) The volunteers didn't hear the city name so they weren't scared.

c) The volunteers became violent and gave the scientists electric shocks.

Answer: a) The volunteers heard the city name but weren't aware of it. And that proves that we're listening even when we think we're not listening.

WORDS AND SMILES

All this talking raises the question of how you ever manage to say anything sensible (after all, this is beyond some people). Well, you wouldn't manage to say anything much if it wasn't for your brain-boggling brain. At the Normal House the boy is having a brain scan to find out why he can talk sense.

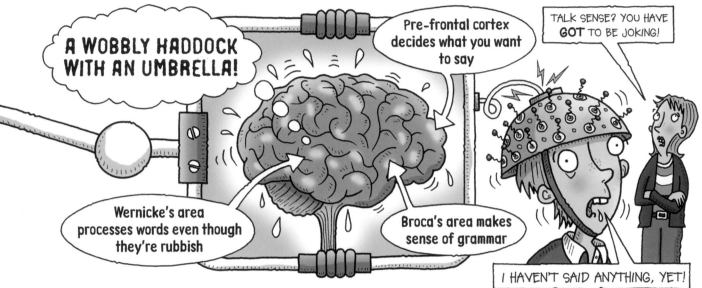

Baffling body language

While your brain is busy talking and listening, another part of your brain is just as busy watching the other person. Just by watching two people you can often figure out who's in charge and what sort of mood they're in – this is called "body language". Just look at the shrinking scientists…

We pick up on these clues and they tell us how to behave to the other person, and this is why you're allowed to enjoy a friendly wrestle with your brother but not with your head teacher. Well, not unless you want to be expelled before you can say "antisocial, irresponsible behaviour".

The expression on a person's face is a big clue to how they're feeling. We'll look at expressions on page 56 – but before then you may like to know that you can make around 7,000 different expressions, and to make them you have to crumple your face muscles in complicated ways. Here's how to smile…

USE YOUR LAVATOR LABII SUPERIORIS MUSCLE TO LIFT YOUR UPPER LIP. AT THE SAME TIME PULL ON THE ANGLE OF YOUR MOUTH WITH YOUR ZYGOMATICUS AND RISORIUS MUSCLES. WITH LUCK YOUR LIPS WILL CURVE UPWARDS AND STRETCH WIDER. SMILING IS AN INTERESTING BEHAVIOURAL RESPONSE – I REALLY MUST TRY IT SOMETIME.

Mind you, if that sounds complicated you ought to know too that smiles can be genuine – or false. If they're false the person is just putting on the smile but not feeling smiley. Here's how to tell the difference…

FALSE SMILE

Eyes don't smile

GRANNY'S KNITTED YOU A NEW JUMPER …

REAL SMILE

Cheeks rise up

AND A PURPLE BOBBLE-HAT FOR YOUR SISTER!

With a genuine smile you can't control your cheek movements – the smile just happens. Why not try it yourself?

GET A MOVE ON!

Balancing on two legs is brain-bogglingly hard – and walking, well, that's simply staggering.

No wonder your cat can't do it! No wonder learning to walk was a toughie. It took you about ten months just to stand up for the first time. Then you probably crash-landed on your bum. You were probably around one before you could toddle – and even that took loads of tottering and tantrums.

It's time for the twins to go to school, but today they're walking with the shrinking scientists. It's not just a healthy way to save fuel – it's a chance for the boffins to study how the children walk. On the way they give the girl's legs a quick scan…

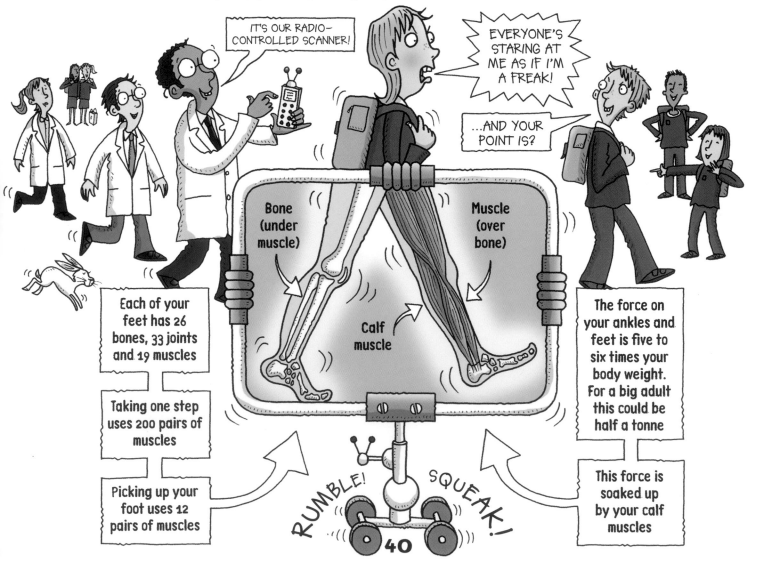

The shrinking scientists have filmed the girl walking. The boy reckons it's a horror film but that's brothers for you…

1 One foot rises and swings forward. Other foot is on the ground. As you walk, thousands of skin flakes rub off against your clothes

2 Front foot hits the ground. Both feet are on the ground now

3 Back foot rises and swings forward. Arms swing to maintain balance and rhythm

(Take care not to step in anything smelly!)

Amazingly enough you spend most of your time – say 80–90 per cent of your journey – balancing on one foot. And that's a lot of balancing considering that you probably take over 8,000 steps a day and plod 160,000 km in your life. No wonder your feet pump out 280 ml of cheesy sweat every day.

The streets are a great place to watch other people walking – just don't do it too obviously or you might get arrested for being a public nuisance.

Adults tend to walk in step. This makes it easier for them to talk without rubbing shoulders. Children don't do this so much

AND RABBITS DON'T CARE.

Bet you never knew!
If you're right-handed, your right leg is probably a bit stronger and longer than your left. (For left-handers it's the other way round.) As a result, when you walk, your right leg takes longer strides and you slowly move to the left. This is why people lost in the desert sometimes wander in circles.

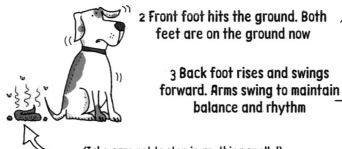

TAKING YOUR HEART AND BRAIN FOR A WALK

It doesn't matter if you stride, sneak, walk, waddle, or trot on tiptoe – you actually need loads of body bits to get about. Let's start with your brainy grey matter and ever-beating body-pump…

You might think that you can amble along, listening to music and chewing gum and daydreaming that a giant wombat has kidnapped your teacher – and so you can. But the reason you can do all this is that your brain is busy looking where you're going and making sure you don't wander into a crocodile's mouth or trip on a pile of elephant poo.

Part of the art of avoiding danger is to judge distance. It helps that you've got two eyes, each with a slightly different view of the world. Your brain fits pictures from your two light-detecting retinas together to create a 3-D image. And you use your memory of how big things are to decide how far away they must be. This skill is very handy for dodging rampaging wildebeest or avoiding lampposts.

And while all this careful calculation is going on, next door to your brain a set of odd-looking tubes are telling you how NOT to fall over…

EEK, I'M GOING TO FALL!

Dangerous demonstration of body balancing – DON'T TRY IT AT HOME!

Fluid-filled semi-circular canals contain motion sensors that pick up changes in the head's position

STAY CALM!

KEEP YOUR HEAD!

YEAH, NOBODY ELSE WANTS IT!

Eventually the children get to school – thanks to the shrinking scientists they're half an hour late. Before they can go to lessons though, our pint-sized pals want to look at the effects of exercise on the boy's heart.

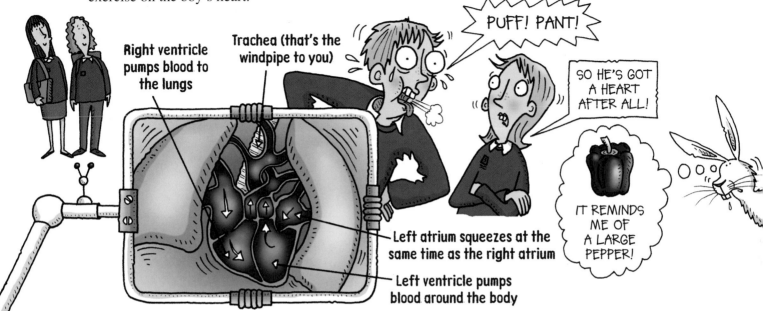

Although your heart only weighs 200 grams, it never takes a holiday or stops for a cup of tea. It beats at least once a second and every minute it works hard enough to send every drop of your blood around your body. By the time you get to 75 years old this marvellous muscle will have squeezed about three billion times. And in all that time your heart never grumbles and never asks for a pay rise. In fact, all it needs is energy from glucose.

Teacher's tea-break teaser

This teaser works best with a sweet-toothed teacher keen on sugar in their tea or coffee. Tap smartly on the staffroom door. When it reluctantly creaks open treat your teacher to a sickly sticky-sweet smile and ask:

I WAS JUST WONDERING WHY YOUR BODY NEEDS GLUCOSE RATHER THAN THE SUGAR YOU PUT IN YOUR TEA?

Answer: Your teacher's tea contains sucrose – a larger molecule than glucose. Sucrose forms crystals rather easily and you wouldn't want a heart full of sugar lumps would you?

BREATH, BLOOD AND BUBBLY LUNGS

Having a heaving heart is vital – but you won't get far without your life-giving lungs. These are two bubbly bags tasked with taking oxygen from the air and sticking it in your blood. They do this with 'bubbles'. Each bubble is a microscopic space called an alveolus (al-ve-o-lus) and you've got a breathtaking 375 million in each lung. Iron your lungs flat and you'll have a wobbly-slimy pink sheet large enough to wallpaper your school hall.

Bet you never knew!

If you've ever tried to blow up a balloon you'll know it needs lots of puff. In 2008, 13-year-old Andrew Dahl blew up 213 balloons in one hour. But he didn't use his mouth – he used … one nostril. Lucky he didn't have a cold then.

44

All these millions of alveoli make a vast surface for oxygen to get into your blood and carbon dioxide to escape back into the air. And all this goes in and out of your body through a series of ever-shrinking tubes. Imagine a leafless tree turned upside down by an antisocial giant with its trunk branching off into ever-smaller twigs and you'll get the idea.

Once it's in your blood, oxygen gets VIP treatment. Instead of being dissolved and hustled away in the raging red river, the lucky oxygen atoms are picked up by red blood cells. Just picture a fleet of luxury red buses.

Each red blood cell contains a protein called haemoglobin that greedily grabs oxygen molecules and keeps them safe as it journeys around your body. I'm not sure if they get to watch a movie and sit on comfy seats, but they're better treated than your food. And on the return trip to the lungs, the waste carbon dioxide enjoys the VIP trip on the red cell buses.

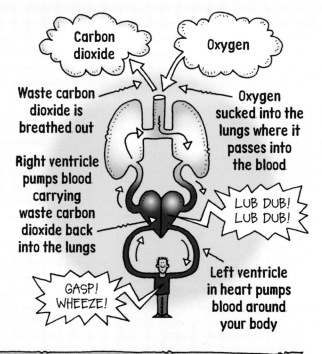

Carbon dioxide

Oxygen

Waste carbon dioxide is breathed out

Oxygen sucked into the lungs where it passes into the blood.

Right ventricle pumps blood carrying waste carbon dioxide back into the lungs

LUB DUB! LUB DUB!

GASP! WHEEZE!

Left ventricle in heart pumps blood around your body

Teacher's tea-break teaser

Rat-a-tat on the staffroom door, and when it squeaks open look your teacher calmly in the eye and enquire…

I WAS WONDERING WHY YOU HAVE DETERGENT IN YOUR LUNGS!

Answer: Believe it or not this is true. Obviously your lung detergent isn't quite the same stuff as washing-up liquid or you'd be blowing bubbles all day… Mind you, your teacher might start frothing at the mouth because they didn't know the answer. But why detergent? Well, your lungs contain water and water is surprisingly sticky stuff. The water molecules pull on each other and the sides of your lungs, making it harder to fill them with air. The detergent in your lungs stops the water sticking to the sides, so you can enjoy a nice deep sigh of relief. I guess you can breathe easily now…

YOUR MIGHTY MUSCLES

Being alive is a deeply moving experience. Why? Well, your muscles are always moving even when you're trying not to move a muscle!

You've actually got three types of muscles:

• Cardiac muscle is the stuff your heart is made from. Good thing it never takes a day off.

• Your smooth muscle works on jobs you do without thinking, such as shifting your food through your guts.

• But when it comes to walking, it's your skeletal muscles that do the legwork.

Your brain might be ever so slightly boggled to discover that you've actually got 638 skeletal muscles and you can move them all if you want to. Fortunately you don't have to work out which order you need to move them. They just do it as soon as you decide what you want to do.

Like all muscles, your mighty moving muscles can only pull and not push. The shrinking scientists are taking a closer look at the boy's muscles.

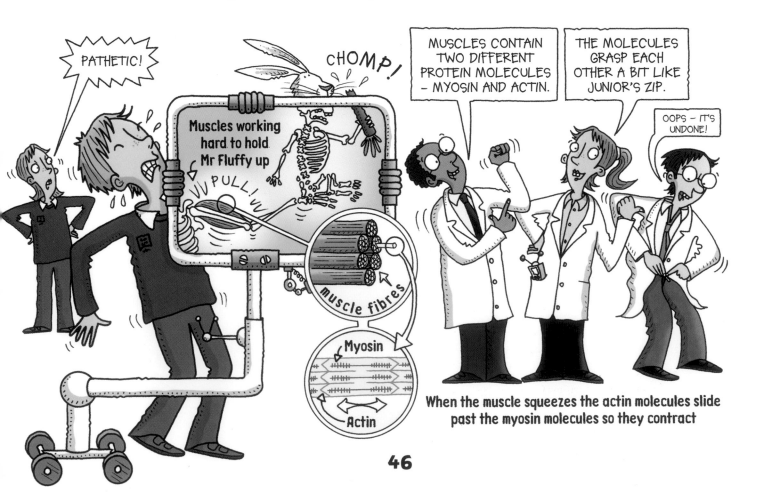

PATHETIC!

CHOMP!

Muscles working hard to hold Mr Fluffy up

↗PULL!

muscle fibres

Myosin

Actin

MUSCLES CONTAIN TWO DIFFERENT PROTEIN MOLECULES – MYOSIN AND ACTIN.

THE MOLECULES GRASP EACH OTHER A BIT LIKE JUNIOR'S ZIP.

OOPS – IT'S UNDONE!

When the muscle squeezes the actin molecules slide past the myosin molecules so they contract

At the risk of complicating things, you've actually got *two* kinds of skeletal muscle:

- Fast-twitch muscles are great for violent action. Imagine you're being chased by a bad-tempered buffalo. Your straining muscles are screaming for more oxygen but your gasping lungs can't get enough. So instead of using oxygen, your fast-twitch muscles convert glucose to lactic acid (the same molecule that you'll find in sour milk).

- Slow-twitch muscles are for those more relaxed moments when you're on the move but you have a chance to breathe too.

Mind you, all the muscles in the world won't get you very far without bones to pull on. The pulling is done on your body's home-made ropes known as tendons. Your tremendous tendons are made of a substance called collagen. Your crucial collagen is made of chains of protein molecules so it's not likely to go PING at an embarrassing moment.

Bone up on numbers QUIZ

All you have to do is put the following body bits in order of which has the most bones.

a) Your skull.

b) Your hands and feet put together.

c) Your spine.

d) Your right hand and arm.

Answers:

b) You have 120 bones in your hands and feet – more than half your total of 206. Not surprising considering all those fingers and toes.

d) You have 32 bones in the right and another 32 in your left hand and arm.

c) Your spine has 26 bones – including seven in your neck.

a) There are 22 bones in your bonce, including eight to protect your brilliant brain from brain bashes.

Bet you never knew!

Along with minerals your bones also contain collagen. This makes them springy so they won't snap like rotten twigs when you go for a nice brisk trot.

47

LOATHSOME LEARNING

Do you leap out of bed yelling, "OH YIPPEE! IT'S SCHOOL TODAY!" Or do you think that school is slightly less fun than having all your teeth pulled out by a mad dentist? Either way, learning is a brain-boggling body job.

Even before you knew you were learning you were learning to walk and talk. By the age of two you could scribble better than any chimp on the planet, and within a year you could draw a face. What's more, you were discovering music and rhyme. Like you, chimps enjoy dancing but by the age of five, you were a better mover than the average ape (and the average dad too). So how on Earth did you manage all this stuff? We've discovered this top-secret baby-training manual hidden under a pile of dribble-splattered bibs.

The Horrible Science Potty Manual for Brighter Babies

Lesson 1: Be a copy-cat
We babies love to copy adults. So if you really want to get ahead in potty training why not make your parents use the potty too? That way you can copy them.

YOUR TURN, DAD!

Lesson 2: Trial and error
We little 'uns love trying things out even if we get them wrong. So if you happen to miss the potty and splash the cat don't scream and cry and throw your rattle about. You just need to try and try and try again. You'll get it right one of these days and your parents can always clear up the mess.

EMPTY!

+ = TRY AGAIN!

Lesson 3: Practice makes perfect
The more you use your new skill the better you get until at last you can do it without trying — without even thinking! So try to use your potty as often as you can, even if you don't actually need it.

CAN'T YOU JUST SIT ON MY LAP LIKE A NORMAL TODDLER?

Er... looks like he did need it!

WAYNE'S FIRST WEE IN A POTTY

OOH, LET'S WATCH AN OLD DVD!

Lesson 4: Think ahead
Make sure your parents aren't filming you. This film could be seriously embarrassing when you get older.

So there you have it. Imitate, learn from your mistakes and keep going – the secret of your early learning success. But just because babies are born learners does that make them smarter than the average ape?

Clever chimps vs talented toddlers QUIZ

IN 2007, GERMAN SCIENTISTS COMPARED THE SKILLS OF 105 TODDLERS WITH 138 APES. WHO PROVED BEST AT...

1 Copying the way an adult human opened a plastic tube?

2 Working out what a human was looking for and pointing to the hidden treat?

Bonus point:
3 In a separate test, a British memory champion took on a chimp at remembering the pattern and order of numbers displayed on a screen. Who won and who was the chump – the champ or the chimp?

Answers:
1 and 2 The talented toddlers trounced the clueless chimps. In test 1 the annoyed apes even tried to bite open the tube after they'd been shown what to do!
3 The clever chimp, seven-year-old Ayumu, beat the human hands and feet down.

So would a chimp make a monkey out of you? Well, one thing's for certain, no chimp on Earth could handle a science test (and they probably wouldn't want to either).

UNLIKE A BRAINY BUNNY!

MIXED-UP MEMORY

Back at the school, the children are preparing for that brain-boggling torture known as the "science test". Being tested by the scaled-down scientists suddenly doesn't seem so bad. Anything is better than quaking at the queasy questions.

Before the test the children have to read a boring science book and learn some facts. (Obviously we're not talking about *this* book. We're talking about the kind of book that keeps headache-pill makers in business.) Meanwhile the shrinking scientists are keen to explore how the brain helps us to read…

THANKS FOR VOLUNTEERING AGAIN!

WELL, HE'S NO GOOD AT READING!

CHEEK!

FASCINATING!

WE CAN READ A LOT INTO THIS.

SCANNER SCREEN SAYS…

Memorization is a bio-electrical process within the cerebrum facilitated by the comprehension of…

Brain sucks in more blood – it needs more glucose and oxygen

Memory areas remember spellings of words

Visual areas try to imagine what the words mean

Heart pumps blood up to brain

PUMP!

Eyeballs scan one chunk of text at a time

PUMP!

CARROTS OF THE WORLD

Bet you never knew!

The curled-up hedgehog rolled down the hill. Faster and faster it rolled until it bounced into the air and splatted in a big pile of cow poo. When you read these words, your mind conjures up the image of the rolling hedgehog and the visual and motion-detection areas of your brain start firing up exactly as if you are seeing it.

50

The brain skill known as "reading" is terribly useful. Every week many people read about 100,000 words – that's five million a year – and forget most of them. But the children need to remember the science facts. So how's it done? We hadn't a clue so we asked the experts…

MEMORY HAS THREE STAGES. WE USE SHORT-TERM MEMORY TO REMEMBER WHAT WE'RE DOING. THIS TAKES THE FORM OF A TEMPORARY CHEMICAL CHANGE IN YOUR BRAIN.

I'LL NEVER REMEMBER ALL THAT!

LONG-TERM MEMORY IS WHAT YOU REMEMBER FOR YEARS. AND WHAT'S THE THIRD STAGE, JUNIOR?

DURRR!

PSST – IT'S RECALL YOU IDIOT!

Recall is remembering what you learnt and making it permanent in your brain. Tests are supposed to help you recall facts. As for memory, just imagine your brain is a brain-boggling forest. Each of your memories is a path. Each path is made of inter-connected brain nerve cells, or neurons. Recalling the memory uses this path again and strengthens the links between the neurons – it's like trampling a forest path until it's clearly marked. Oh well, it's better than being "lost in thought".

Back at school the girl is struggling to recall the facts…

Memory centres working overtime

Vision becomes concentrated on what she's doing

Tongue sticks out of mouth. Some people do this when concentrating to hold their tongue still. Tongue movements can distract the brain

ER, IS IT CEREBRUM OR CEREBELLUM?

Different bits of a memory are stored in different parts of your brain. That's why you can often remember someone's face but not the person's name – or their name but not their face.

IT MAKES YOU THINK...

While the twins are finishing off their science test let's have a quiet think about your brain. I mean, I bet you never think about how your brain is split in two. But what does it mean? Is this why you're in two minds about everything?

It's actually quite a sensible arrangement. In most people, each side of the brain has a different job. Usually the left side deals with facts and words and maths, and the right side is more interested in art and music. But hopefully both sides work together fairly happily. Let's see what happens when Junior tries to sing...

THIS IS A SONG ABOUT MY BRAIN... I NEED TWO HALVES TO KEEP ME SANE...

OH SHUT UP, JUNIOR!

Oh dear – he sounds like a cats' karaoke contest

AND WHEN I TYPE, MY RIGHT BRAIN CAN REMEMBER WHERE THE KEYS ARE EVEN THOUGH MY LEFT BRAIN HASN'T A CLUE.

TAP! TAP! TAP!

View of Junior's brain from the back

His left brain works on the words

Junior's right brain works on the tune

The fact that you've basically got two brains explains why you're right or left-handed. Each side of your brain looks after the opposite side of your body. So if you're right-handed it means that your left-brain is in charge. For left-handers it's the opposite way round.

Most people use one eye more than the other for seeing. You can find which eye you use more by holding your finger at arm's length in front of a distant object. Now close and open each eye in turn. The finger will seem to move to the side when you do this – but it will jump most when you close your "stronger eye". And guess what? It's usually the side controlled by the bossy side of your brain. That means if you're right-handed your right eye is probably your stronger eye.

Bet you never knew!

Imagine a mad maths teacher gave you a 200-digit number and asked which other number can be multiplied 13 times to get it. You need to work out that sum without a calculator. Would you faint or cry or run for the hills? In 2007 Alexis Lemaire worked out the correct answer – 2,407,899,893,032,210 ... in just 70.2 seconds. I bet he had a planet-sized left brain.

Silly brain QUIZ

Here's your chance to test your brain-boggling brain cells. Some bits of your brain and spinal cord have silly names – but which of these names sound too silly to be true?

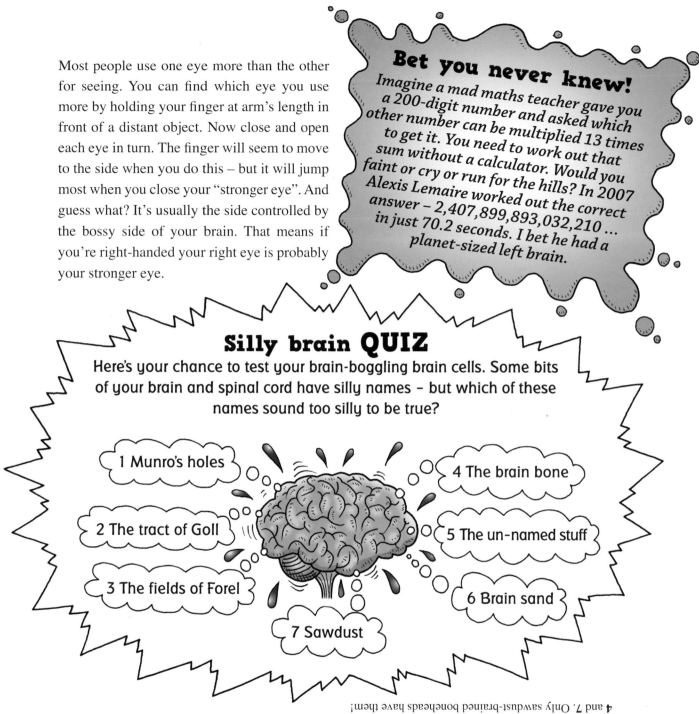

1 Munro's holes

2 The tract of Goll

3 The fields of Forel

4 The brain bone

5 The un-named stuff

6 Brain sand

7 Sawdust

True answers:
1 They're in the spaces under your cerebrum.
2 You'll find this bundle of nerves in your spinal cord.
3 They're close to your hypothalamus.
5 It's actually a Latin name (substantia innominata) but this is what it means.
6 No, it's not what teachers have for brains – it's minerals that build up in your brain as you get older.

False answers:
4 and 7. Only sawdust-brained boneheads have them!

53

GROOVY GAMES

At long last the bell goes and the children run off to do what they've wanted to do all day. PLAY! And the shrinking scientists are thrilled too. They reckon that playing builds the kids' brains. But are they right? Well, here's the scientific proof …

Consider this – the smarter the animal, the more it plays. This is true – I mean, when was the last time you saw cheerful crickets playing cricket? How many snakes actually play snakes and ladders? Who ever heard of a frog playing leapfrog? But young mammals such as kittens and puppies have bigger brains and they love to play. And young chimps even make a special face when they want to have fun.

But compared with a crazy kitten or playful puppy you're a long-playing player. Most mammals give up playing in a year or two as they grow up – but humans carry on for years. And…

Here's what scientists think about play…

A science report by Junior

According to scientists like what I am, play is about finding out more about what you can do. This is true – I never knew I could stretch chewing gum from my teeth to the length of my arm until I tried. And what's more, I'm getting better at kicking a ball up and bouncing it on my head – OH NO! I've broken the staffroom window!

54

Discovering what you can do is very important. Just imagine that you had never played – ever. You would have missed out on important learning experiences. For example…

You wouldn't know how to make a paper dart. Or catch a ball with one hand. Or flick a low-flying pea into a teacher's soup. What's more, when you play you use the same techniques as when you're learning – that's to say you repeat the experience and try new games that might not work. No wonder you learn when you play. Tell that to your teacher next time you get told off for having fun!

… BUT PLAY IS AN IMPORTANT LEARNING EXPERIENCE THAT HELPS IN THE GRADUAL DEVELOPMENT OF LIFE SKILLS THROUGHOUT CHILDHOOD… MISS!

But play offers a bigger brain-boggling benefit. Since you're not in a lesson you are free to have creative ideas. And then you have loads of fun trying out your exciting new ideas. To show what happens we've challenged our creative Horrible Science artist to combine four different images …

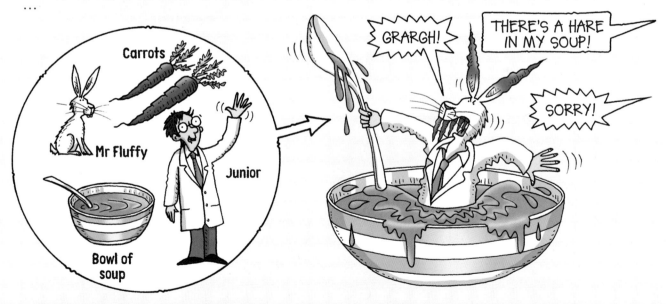

WOW! You'd need to scoff a lot of smelly cheese to have a nightmare like that! But creativity makes it easy. Why not try combining four images in your own weird drawing? And the same creativity that makes play fun can create new music, new ideas in science or even great works of literature like this book.

FEELING AND FIGHTING

Rage and joy can boggle your brain. But if we humans had no feelings we'd be as boring as robots …

ME – BORING? THE CHEEK OF IT!

HE SAID ROBOTS NOT RABBITS!

According to scientists, you, me and everyone on Planet Earth has six main emotions that show as different expressions on our faces. And we humans are great at checking expressions on other people's faces to work out how they feel. I bet you can spot the six emotions on the shrinking scientists' faces…

YOU'LL GET NO MORE CHOCCIES UNTIL NEXT WEEK...	Surprise / Anger	BUT I'VE DONE NOTHING WRONG!
YOU CAN HAVE A NICE HEALTHY CARROT...	Disgust	HEY THAT'S MINE!
OH ALL RIGHT, HERE'S SOME DIFFERENT CHOCCIES...	Joy	OOH, GOODY!
OH DEAR – THEY'RE LAXATIVE CHOCCIES FOR CONSTIPATION...	Fear / Sad	PARP!

Mind you, there's a bit more to feelings than just six emotions. I mean, what about guilt or pride or satisfaction? Scientists think these might be mixtures of the main emotions but if so we must be pretty mixed-up. Maybe that's why sometimes we don't know what we're feeling...

As you grow up you collect lots of little triggers that switch on feelings in your brain. One trigger might be a particular smell – and I can prove it. Imagine a smell (no, you don't have to make it). Chances are that the smell reminds you of a place and the way you felt at the time. Inside your brain, nerves from the whiff receptors in your nose connect with your limbic system – a part of your brain that shapes your feelings and helps to recall memories.

The smell he thinks of reminds him of the day he put his potty on his head.

Pain is another sensation that gets your feelings going. If you've ever been stung by a wasp you know how bad it feels. In your brain, the memory of the pain gets linked to your memory of the wasp and you might feel scared of wasps in the future.

Bet you never knew!

Spare a thought for US scientist Justin Schmidt. This brave boffin allowed himself to be stung by 78 vicious insects to create a sting pain scorecard. Bees and wasps score 2 but that's nothing...

Also at 2, a sting from a bald-faced hornet is like getting your hand mashed in a revolving door – Ouch!

Up one at 3, a red harvester ant sting is like someone pulling out your ingrowing-toenail ... with a drill. Yeeouch!

Far worse at 4, is the pepsis wasp sting – it's like a violent electric shock and all you can do is scream. Aggggh!

But the top scorer with 4+ is the bullet ant. A sting from this creepy creepy-crawly is like walking over burning charcoal with a huge nail hammered into your heel.

YARRRRRRRGH!

Maybe bees and wasps aren't so bad...

HOW TO LAUGH YOUR HEAD OFF

By the time you were four months old you could do something that every human (except teachers) can do. You could laugh. It's so basic that some animals do it too. Here's how to laugh chimp-style...

1 Get into role – grab a banana, loosen up and let your arms dangle

2 Push your lips forward. Make sure you show your teeth

3 Make a panting sound like this!

4 Gradually up the volume and jump up and down until someone tells you to shut up

Back at school the boy gets a bad case of the giggles when the school bully trips over Mr Fluffy and goes flying...

Seizing the moment, the shrinking scientists quickly scan the boy's brain to find out what's going on. It looks as if the boy's funny bone has been well and truly tickled...

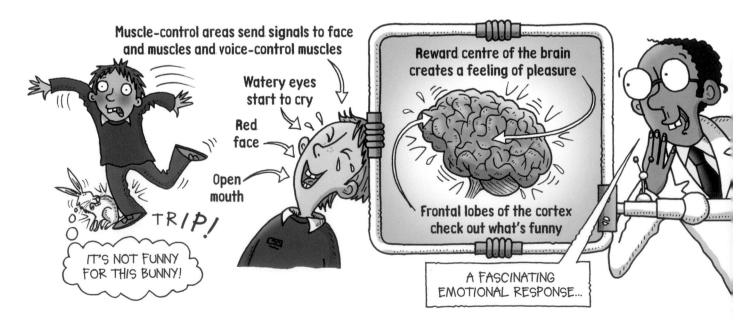

58

You know what makes you laugh, but have you ever wondered *why* you laugh? Well, according to scientists who take this sort of thing seriously, laughing is a way to show relief. They say that while you're laughing at something odd or silly you're secretly relieved that it's not dangerous – do you agree? Well, it might explain why a person making a parachute jump might laugh like a drain when their parachute opens but if the parachute doesn't open they might cry instead. Babies laugh when you clap your hands or lift them up or play peek-a-boo with them. It's their way of showing relief because you're not as scary as you look. But when you laugh at someone it's like saying that they're odd but harmless. That's two insults for the price of one. No wonder most people don't like being laughed at. And no wonder the school bully turns nasty when the boy laughs at him … again!

Now the shrinking scientists get the chance to discover the effects of rage on bodies. A lot of what's going on is based in part of the brain called the amygdala (a-mig-da-la).

HORMONE HAVOC

There's more to losing your rag than boggled brain cells. Whilst your neurons are busily buzzing, the rest of your body gets in a state because your emotions release hormones.

Hormones are chemical messengers that order certain body bits to do certain jobs. For example, hormones make your guts squirt digestive juices. Hormones are made in glands (a bit like your sweat and salivary glands – only instead of dripping sweat or squirting spit they dribble hormones into your blood). The glands are found in different parts of your body. Here are the main glands you need to know about…

Glands are controlled by – guess what? More hormones from the pituitary

YOUR BROTHER'S GOING TO GET THUMPED!

OH DEAR!

GRRRRR!

1 Hypothalamus

2 Pituitary controlled by hypothalamus (remember that brain bit from page 12?)

3 Thyroid controls the speed your body produces energy

4 Adrenal glands

5 Pancreas – makes insulin to reduce the amount of glucose in your blood

6 Testes – see page 76 (girls have ovaries)

7 Carrotoid gland – uses carrot juice to make whiskers*

*Just joking!

When you're angry, the main hormone involved is called adrenaline. And right now the amazing adrenaline is playing havoc with the boy's body…

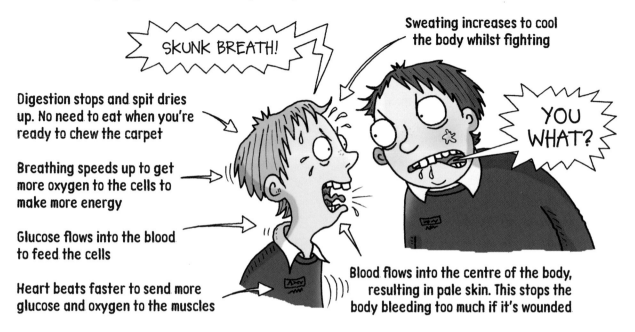

SKUNK BREATH!

Sweating increases to cool the body whilst fighting

Digestion stops and spit dries up. No need to eat when you're ready to chew the carpet

YOU WHAT?

Breathing speeds up to get more oxygen to the cells to make more energy

Glucose flows into the blood to feed the cells

Heart beats faster to send more glucose and oxygen to the muscles

Blood flows into the centre of the body, resulting in pale skin. This stops the body bleeding too much if it's wounded.

But the bully is bigger than the boy and so the boy's a bit scared too. His cortex is sending danger signals to his amygdala. At this point it's not certain that the two boys will fight. After all, the sensible cortex can still tell them that fighting generally ends with someone getting hurt. This is why an angry human or animal will often back down without fighting. A good way to do this is (if you're human) is to burst into tears – most of us feel protective towards someone in distress. This instinct is designed to care for babies but it works with older people too.

But simmering down after a strop is easier said than done. After all, your body is still raging with anger hormones. Often people take out their temper with a displacement activity. This means doing something that doesn't need doing, like kicking a tin can.

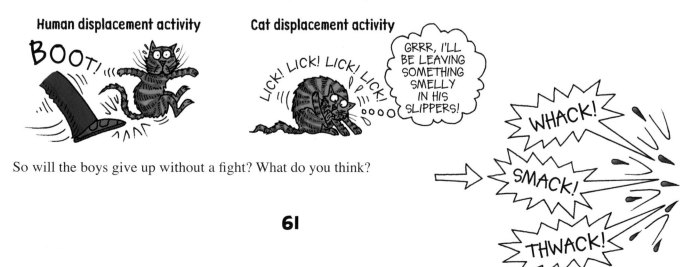

Human displacement activity

BOOT!

Cat displacement activity

LICK! LICK! LICK! LICK!

GRRR, I'LL BE LEAVING SOMETHING SMELLY IN HIS SLIPPERS!

WHACK!

SMACK!

THWACK!

So will the boys give up without a fight? What do you think?

NASTY NERVES

The boy, the school bully and the shrinking scientists have been summoned to the head teacher's office to answer some awkward questions about the fight and the broken staffroom window from page 54...

Things look difficult – but for the scientists it's a golden opportunity to study the effects of stress on the body. The boys feel stress because their bodies are fired up to fight or escape but they can't do either. After all they can't beat up the head teacher and run for their lives.

Here's what stress is doing to the boy's body...

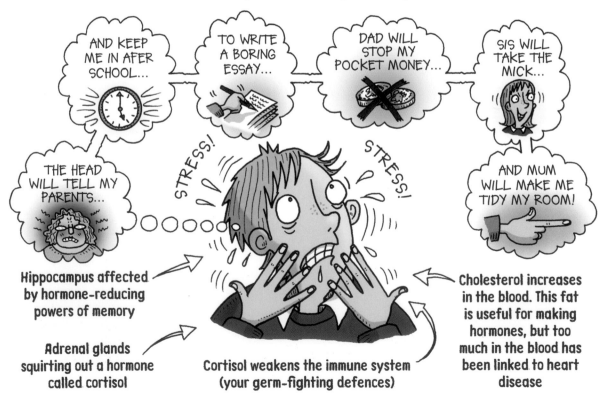

Hippocampus affected by hormone-reducing powers of memory

Adrenal glands squirting out a hormone called cortisol

Cortisol weakens the immune system (your germ-fighting defences)

Cholesterol increases in the blood. This fat is useful for making hormones, but too much in the blood has been linked to heart disease

Stress isn't exactly a bundle of laughs but your body often makes things worse. Deep inside your boggling brain your cortex, amygdala and memory are busy winding each other up …

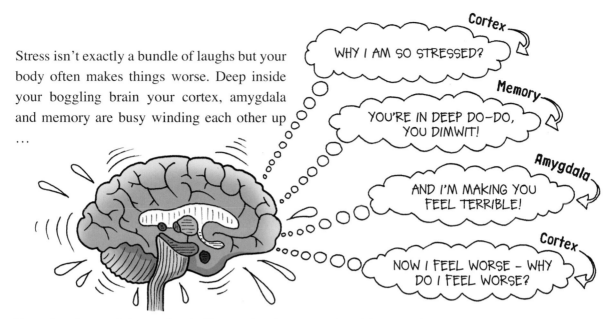

Round and round they go, winding each other up and making you feel worse. Luckily, your clever cortex is in control and it's possible to talk yourself into a more relaxed frame of mind. (Just don't talk to yourself loudly in public or you won't be allowed on public transport.) Junior is trying to take our advice – by calming his cortex he can damp down his cortisol levels and feel better. Trouble is, it doesn't quite work…

HURTING AND HEALING

It's hard to live a normal life and not get hurt. Life is full of bumps and bashes, and even the most accident-proof person picks up a few cuts and bruises. Some people pick up a lot more.

Bruise due to broken blood vessels bleeding under the skin

Nosebleed caused by broken blood vessel

Keeping head down stops blood from flowing into mouth

I FINK MY EYEBALL'S COME OUT.

BY DOSE IS OUT OF SHAPE.

THIS NICE COLD SPONGE WILL CONSTRICT THE DAMAGED BLOOD VESSELS AND STOP THE BLEEDING.

Pressing the soft part of the schnozzle for ten minutes will stop the bleeding by allowing a blood clot to form

WHAT A LITTLE DRIP!

The two boys have been lucky. Some people suffer far worse injuries. And some injuries are far, far, far worse. We checked on Dr Grimgrave's fracture and muscle-damage clinic to find some really serious cases…

THERE ARE TWO WAYS TO BREAK A BONE – HIT IT OR TWIST IT – BUT ONLY ONE CAUSE. THESE IDIOTS IGNORE SENSIBLE SAFETY WARNINGS FROM THEIR LONG-SUFFERING DOCTOR. THEN THEY COME TO ME MOANING AND GROANING. WHAT DO THEY EXPECT ME TO DO – HEAL THEM? GRR – I'M ONLY A DOCTOR!

Dr Grimgrave the world's most dismal doc

64

1 Broken rib – this can be caused by laughing and crying. Well, you won't catch Dr G doing much of either...

2 Whiplash injury – caused by a sudden shaking of the neck. It can break apart one of the joints between the neck bones (vertebrae)

3 Broken collar bone (or clavicle as Dr G calls it)

4 Colles' fracture just above the wrist caused by falling on your hands

5 Femur (thigh bone) with break in the neck of the bone

6 Broken ankle caused by a violent twist (it's actually a break at the end of the two lower leg bones – tibia or fibula)

These patients have to be very patient and let their injuries heal. At least they'll get a nice break (ha, ha). But there's better news on the next two pages. Your brain-boggling body actually heals itself …

65

HOPEFUL HEALING

You may not be into DO IT YOURSELF repairs, but thank goodness your body is. If it wasn't for your bod's habit of healing itself you wouldn't last longer than your next cut or cold.

Let's start with clotting – well there's a good opportunity here. The shrinking scientists take a look at the boy's injured nose.

1. Blood drips from broken blood vessel

2. Bits of cells called platelets try to plug the gap

3. Protein fibres create a net

4. Platelets and red blood cells get stuck in the net

5. Body cells squeeze to tighten area of wound

THIRTEEN DIFFERENT CHEMICALS ARE INVOLVED IN CLOTTING.

GUH?

NOW HE'S A LITTLE CLOT!

In a few hours the surface of the wound hardens to a nice crusty scab. Meanwhile new cells grow around the wound to seal it off from the germ-laden air.

Bet you never knew!

One wound your body can't heal is a chopped-off head. In 1905, French medic Dr Beaurieux was testing a murderer's beheaded bonce. The doctor spoke the man's name and the head's eyes opened. The doc repeated the name and the head's eyes opened again – but the third call had no reaction. It looks like death follows in 30 seconds. Oh well, I guess it helps to get a-head in medicine.

HE WAS A REAL HEAD CASE.

I'M FEELING HACKED OFF!

Sometimes healing doesn't go according to plan. If a wound is large and can't heal fast enough to keep germs out, an army of fibroblast (fi-bro-blast) cells moves into the gap and seals it with collagen. (Remember that precious protein from page 47?) This covers the wound but you get an ugly scar instead of nice new skin. Got any of these?

If you're ever unlucky enough to break a bone, your body works hard to put things right. Here's an X-ray from the time Junior broke his funny bone trying to give Mr Fluffy a ride down a steep hill in a supermarket trolley.

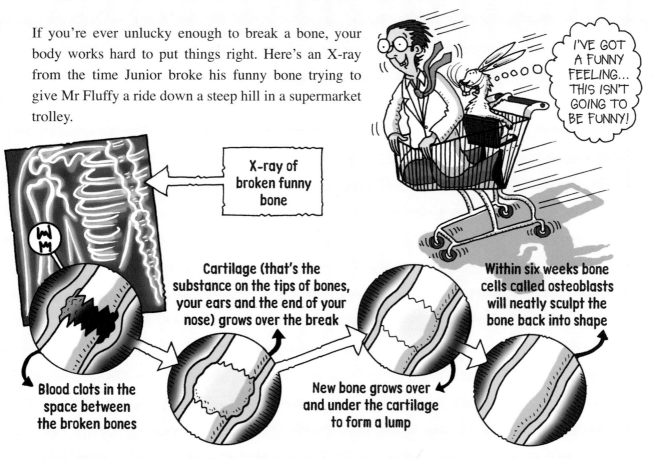

I'VE GOT A FUNNY FEELING... THIS ISN'T GOING TO BE FUNNY!

X-ray of broken funny bone

Cartilage (that's the substance on the tips of bones, your ears and the end of your nose) grows over the break

Within six weeks bone cells called osteoblasts will neatly sculpt the bone back into shape

Blood clots in the space between the broken bones

New bone grows over and under the cartilage to form a lump

Isn't that great? All doctors have to do is to put the bone in a sling, plaster or splint to hold the broken bits together whilst they heal! Sometimes they need to use pins for this job – but all the time the body is doing the repair job.

And what's more, every minute your body is trying its hardest to keep germs out. Remember how spit contained that lovely lysozyme stuff that bumped off bacteria? It's found in tears and snot too. If germs squirm into your nose and mouth they risk getting stuck in the snot and eventually gulped down into the acid bath in your tum. And your ear holes are no more inviting – bacteria get stuck in the gunky wax. But they can consider themselves lucky. Lucky compared to the unlucky germs that dare to venture inside your body fortress…

YOUR DEADLY DISEASE DEFENCES

The inside of your body is every germ's ideal holiday destination. It's warm and cosy and full of good things to eat – even if you never invited them for tea. Some germs slither through open wounds in your skin. Others gurgle down your throat and dive through your stomach acid without getting dissolved whilst others wriggle up your nostrils. They include brutal bacteria, awful amoebae and vicious viruses. Much smaller than bacteria, viruses try to hijack your cells and force them to make copies of themselves that get into more cells and so on.

Let's imagine you're a bacterium*. You've managed to creep past the body's outer defences and now you and your microbe mates are greedily guzzling the cells. All of a sudden nearby blood vessels widen and the human feels heat and swelling – it's called inflammation. As the vessels widen, out tumbles the most ruthless, deadiest army in the known universe … white blood cells. And it's no use running up the white flag – these guys take no prisoners. Within minutes a white blood cell is reaching out its long slippery slimy arms to swallow you up and digest you ALIVE!

*One microbe is a bacterium – more than one are bacteria.

Yet more white blood cells arrive from the lymphatic (lim-fat-ic) system (this is the body's network of drainage tubes). The newcomers are armed with proteins called antibodies designed to stick to the antigens on the bacteria. Tagging the germs helps other white blood cells find and destroy them

Beastly bacterium guzzling body cells

Macrophage – type of white blood cell designed to swallow up germs and other intruders

CHOMP!

MUNCH!

ERK!

GUZZLE!

MUNCH!

68

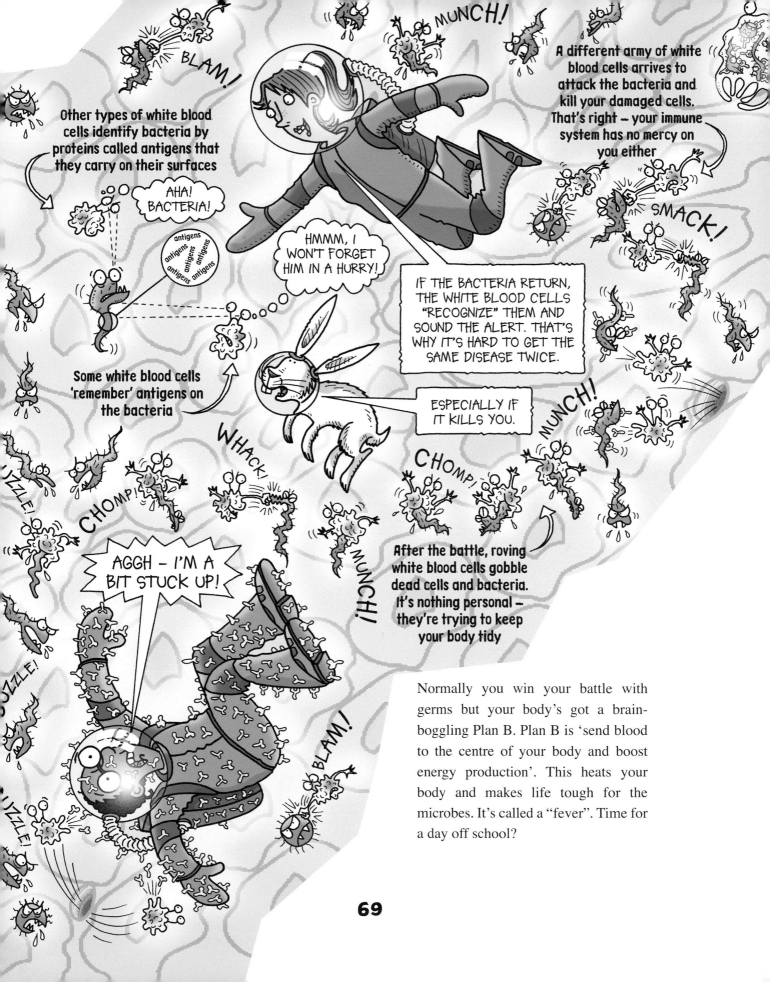

Other types of white blood cells identify bacteria by proteins called antigens that they carry on their surfaces

AHA! BACTERIA!

antigens antigens antigens antigens antigens antigens

Some white blood cells 'remember' antigens on the bacteria

BLAM!

MUNCH!

A different army of white blood cells arrives to attack the bacteria and kill your damaged cells. That's right – your immune system has no mercy on you either

SMACK!

HMMM, I WON'T FORGET HIM IN A HURRY!

IF THE BACTERIA RETURN, THE WHITE BLOOD CELLS "RECOGNIZE" THEM AND SOUND THE ALERT. THAT'S WHY IT'S HARD TO GET THE SAME DISEASE TWICE.

ESPECIALLY IF IT KILLS YOU.

WHACK!

CHOMP!

CHOMP!

MUNCH!

MUNCH!

After the battle, roving white blood cells gobble dead cells and bacteria. It's nothing personal – they're trying to keep your body tidy

AGGH – I'M A BIT STUCK UP!

BLAM!

Normally you win your battle with germs but your body's got a brain-boggling Plan B. Plan B is 'send blood to the centre of your body and boost energy production'. This heats your body and makes life tough for the microbes. It's called a "fever". Time for a day off school?

69

TERRIBLE TEENS

At last school is over – but the shrinking scientists are keen to continue their mission. This time they'll be using their newly invented Body Accelerating Development machine to speed up body changes in the twins. The scientists want to study what happens when the twins become teenagers. The twins can't wait to wear cool clothes and stay up really late…

Under the machine's scary light the children start to change. Their bodies grow and in a few moments they age five years. The shrinking scientists eagerly check out the children's rapidly dividing cells…

IT'S A B.A.D. MACHINE!

WHY? WHAT'S WRONG WITH IT?

EEK!

1 Body cell (from page 8)

2 The nucleus contains 23 pairs of chromosomes

3 The chromosomes copy themselves, pulling apart along tiny ropes that extend like telescopic rods

4 The bits and pieces of the cell – such as the mitochondria – go to one side or another

5 The cell pulls in two

If your cells died off without dividing first, in about 200 days there wouldn't be much left of you except your teeth, bones, brain and nerves. But when you're a teenager your cells divide much faster than they die off – so you get bigger.

One body bit that doesn't grow too much is your head. When you were born you needed a big head to contain your brain-boggling brain. That's why little kids have big heads sitting on top of their little bodies.

Dare you discover
how to weigh your teacher's head?

I'm sure your teacher would be delighted to try this test devised by *New Scientist* magazine...

EH?

You will need:

Your brain. That's all. There's NO WAY you can try this experiment so you'll have to imagine it. Scientists call this a "thought experiment".

What you do:

1 Give your teacher a haircut. You want to weigh their *head*, not their hair.

SNIP! SNIP! SNIP! SNIP!

K-SPLOOP!

2 Fill a bucket to the brim with freezing cold water – as close to 0°C as you can get. Place the bucket in a bowl. Lower your teacher head first into the bucket. Don't keep their head underwater for *too* long!

SPLOOSH!

3 Weigh the water displaced (pushed aside into the bowl) by your teacher's head. Since the head – including the brain – is more than 70 per cent water it will weigh roughly the same as the displaced water.

4.5 KG?

MAYBE A BIT LESS AS HER BRAIN'S SO SMALL.

GRRR!

You should find:

One litre of water weighs 1 kg at 0°C and your teacher's head ought to push aside around 4.5 litres. This proves that your teacher's head weighs 4.5 kg – the weight of three large bags of sugar. And that's quite a lot to carry around all day. Maybe your teacher could do with a long holiday?

CRUCIAL CHANGES

If getting bigger was all you did as a teenager, life would be a lot simpler. But your body and brain and life are all changing fast. Both boys and girls grow thicker hair under their arms and in other unmentionable areas. Girls put on fat around their hips and need to wear bras. Boys get bigger muscles and larger chests and wispy hairs on their chins. A boy's voice deepens as his larynx grows. At first their muscle control isn't too good and their new deep voice gets squeaky at awkward moments…

The scientists are interested in the spots and they can't wait to investigate…

*Pus = dead bacteria and white blood cells. It's nothing to do with pussycats with sore paws.

The cause of all these brain-boggling changes is found in the brain. Triggered by your genes (see page 74), the pituitary starts to squirt hormones. There's growth hormone (you don't need a Nobel Prize to work out what this one does). And there are hormones to turn you into an adult – a process called puberty.

A boy's pituitary pumps out a hormone that tells his testes to make testosterone – that's the hormone that gives them bigger muscles and a deeper voice. Thanks to this handy hormone even if the lazy boy exercises less than his sister he still grows bigger muscles. Women make testosterone too – but not enough to turn them into slobbish blokes who burp in public and never change their pants.

WELL, ONCE A YEAR... MAYBE!

PONG!

BURP! YEAH, WHATEVER.

Meanwhile, in the girl the same pituitary hormone is busily triggering her ovaries to make oestrogen (ee-stro-gen) and progesterone. These hormones make her look like a woman – and control the release of eggs in her ovaries. For the next 35 or so years she'll produce a microscopic egg roughly every 28 days and bleed it out if it's not needed to make a baby. It's called the menstrual cycle.

If scary hormones and squirting spots weren't enough, the poor teenager has to cope with a changing brain. Somehow they've got to change from depending on adults for info to solving problems on their own. And all their time their brains are coping with exams, getting interested in the opposite sex, and parents who don't understand them. Who says teenagers have it easy?

ME!

SHUT UP!

Bet you never knew!
Scientists reckon that teenagers' brains find it harder to judge how other people feel by looking at their expressions. And they also find it harder to judge risks. Is that why teenagers ignore their parents and take silly risks?

GENIUS GENES

The story so far – the shrinking scientists have turned the boy and girl into teenagers. Meanwhile their parents are in shock at their shocking teenage behaviour.

It's easy to blame the terrible teenagers' tearaway hormones – but the shrinking scientists are studying a deeper cause for all this teenage turmoil.

In most of your body's 50 million million cells there's a nucleus, and in all of these there are chromosomes. Each crucial chromosome is a cunningly coiled molecule of DNA (or deoxyribonucleic [de-oxy-ri-bo-new-klee-ic] acid if you fancy yourself as a budding boffin).

DNA is brain-boggling stuff. Your chromosomes are like a manual for making a new you, with instructions for everything from hair colour to the shape of your little toe. This means your DNA is unique to you and even a speck of a cell or a pinprick of blood containing your DNA can tell people who you are.

Three interesting DNA facts that hardly anyone knows

WOW! COOL!

1 If you wanted to read out your code it would take you 100 years (that's assuming you didn't stop to sleep, eat or go to the toilet).

2 The complete molecule can be 5 cm long, which raises the interesting question of how it manages to fit inside a cell thousands of times smaller. The trick is to coil it in the chromosome, but getting 23 pairs of chromosomes into a cell is still like stuffing your suitcase with 7.4 km of smelly socks.

3 If you took all the DNA from every cell of every person on Earth and laid it in a line, it would stretch to the next galaxy.

The shrinking scientists have shrunk down to take an incredibly close look at one of the girl's DNA molecules…

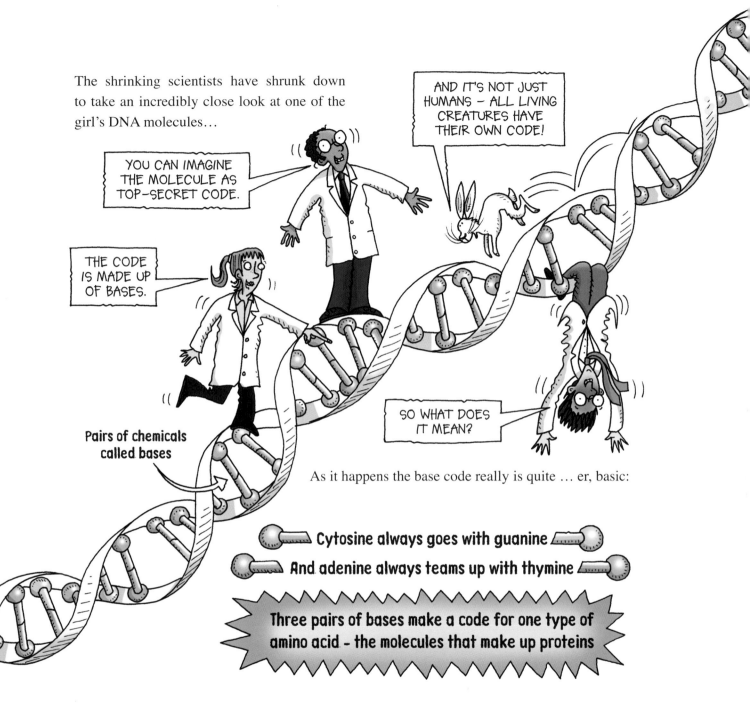

YOU CAN IMAGINE THE MOLECULE AS TOP-SECRET CODE.

AND IT'S NOT JUST HUMANS – ALL LIVING CREATURES HAVE THEIR OWN CODE!

THE CODE IS MADE UP OF BASES.

Pairs of chemicals called bases

SO WHAT DOES IT MEAN?

As it happens the base code really is quite … er, basic:

Cytosine always goes with guanine

And adenine always teams up with thymine

Three pairs of bases make a code for one type of amino acid - the molecules that make up proteins

It's great to have your own code – but on their own they're as much use as software without a computer. What you need is a protein-making machine that uses the codes to build body bits and that's exactly what you've got. In fact you've got trillions of them. They're called ribosomes and molecule-by-molecule they create the proteins that make your cells. What's more, before you were born, they made you. Want to know how? All will be revealed in the next chapter!

A BIT OF BREEDING

There are two types of humans – male and female. OK, so you knew that. But I bet you never knew that the BIG DECISION to make you a boy or girl was taken by your chromosomes?

If you're a boy you have one Y chromosome that you got from your dad and one X chromosome from your mum.

If you're a girl you have two X chromosomes – one from your mum and one from your dad.

I'VE GOT TWO X CHROMOSOMES.

WHY?

NO X!

WHAT HAVE EGGS GOT TO DO WITH IT?

YOU'LL FIND OUT ON THE NEXT PAGE, DURR!

And you guessed it, it's the Y chromosome with its male genes that makes the difference between being a boy and being a girl.

But how your chromosomes got together and decided to make you is another story. It's a tale about sperm and eggs. Every day an adult male can make 350 million sperm in his testes. But getting the sperm to the egg is the most difficult job in the world.

JOIN THE GREAT EGG RACE!

Are you a fit, healthy, ambitious young sperm?

Do you have 23 chromosomes to share?

Are you eager for adventure, excitement and the near certainty of a violent death?

1 You cross the starting line with at least 70 million sperm. Only one of you can win.

GO!

2 You swim with your beating tail. You'll have to swim fast because 1,000 tail beats will only get you 10 mm.

BEAT!

3 Dodge the dreaded white blood cell patrols. If they catch you they'll eat you.

4 You need to find the fallopian tubes and home in on the warmth of the egg. If there's no egg you'll die in a couple of days.

HERE IT IS!

5 When you find the egg you've got to act fast to dissolve its cell wall. The other sperm will help ... but after that it's every sperm for himself.

6 The first sperm in sets off a chemical locking device in the egg to keep the other sperm out.

Out of the 70 million starters nearly all the sperm get lost or killed on the way. Only 100 of them make it as far as the egg – assuming there is one. The effort of getting there is like you trying to swim 11 km ... through jelly. And the unlucky 99 that reach the egg and don't get inside are scoffed by hungry white blood cells. Come to think of it, you are unbelievably lucky. A male human can make billions of sperm. You're descended from the one that made it.

Bet you never knew!
Non-identical twins, like the children in this book, are descended from two sperm and two eggs that developed at the same time. Identical twins started off as one egg that split in half after a sperm came to visit.

THE GREAT GENE-SWAP GAME

At last they've teamed up and you might think that the sperm and egg would want to relax and maybe watch TV – but they don't. They play a game – but we're not talking scrabble or monopoly. They want to play gene swap. It's a chromosome game that will decide what you look like.

The sperm and egg were made by a clever kind of cell division that produced four cells each with 23 chromosomes. But the genes were shuffled too. And that means you can't have a copy of your parents' chromosomes so it's impossible for you to look exactly like either of your parents or your embarrassing brother/sister.

THANK GOODNESS FOR THAT!

Bet you never knew!

Most of the scientific work with genes has been done with fruit flies and on the way scientists have bred extra-stupid fruit flies (yes, even denser than the average fruit fly) using genes with silly nicknames like "cabbage", "radish" and "turnip". And no, they weren't used to make your brother's brain so stop grinning and carry on reading!

WHICH ONE OF YOU IS CARROT?

The sperm and egg play the gene-swap game because they have 46 chromosomes and two sets of genes between them. And they need to sort out which genes take charge of your appearance. Here's how they do it…

Dare you discover
the eerie eyeball colour game?

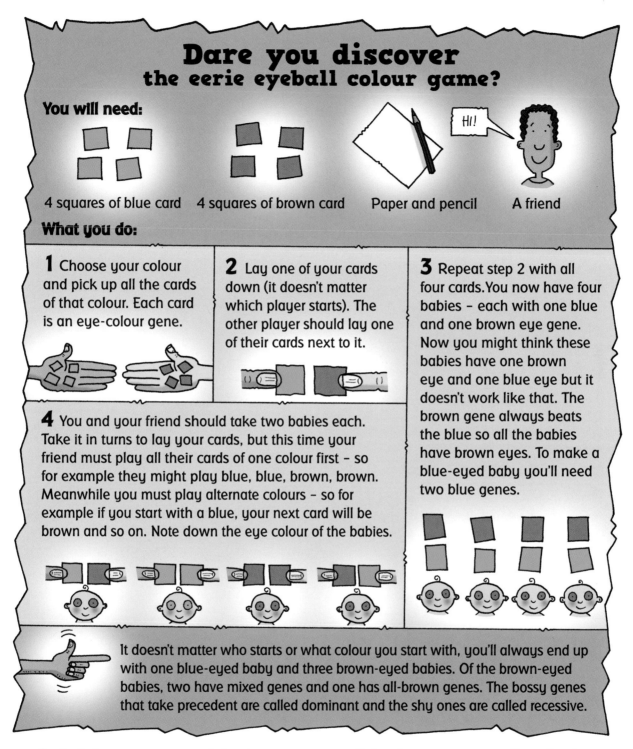

You will need:

4 squares of blue card

4 squares of brown card

Paper and pencil

HI!

A friend

What you do:

1 Choose your colour and pick up all the cards of that colour. Each card is an eye-colour gene.

2 Lay one of your cards down (it doesn't matter which player starts). The other player should lay one of their cards next to it.

3 Repeat step 2 with all four cards. You now have four babies – each with one blue and one brown eye gene. Now you might think these babies have one brown eye and one blue eye but it doesn't work like that. The brown gene always beats the blue so all the babies have brown eyes. To make a blue-eyed baby you'll need two blue genes.

4 You and your friend should take two babies each. Take it in turns to lay your cards, but this time your friend must play all their cards of one colour first – so for example they might play blue, blue, brown, brown. Meanwhile you must play alternate colours – so for example if you start with a blue, your next card will be brown and so on. Note down the eye colour of the babies.

It doesn't matter who starts or what colour you start with, you'll always end up with one blue-eyed baby and three brown-eyed babies. Of the brown-eyed babies, two have mixed genes and one has all-brown genes. The bossy genes that take precedent are called dominant and the shy ones are called recessive.

So that's how your genes sorted out your appearance. But so far you were one cell smaller than a pinhead and thinner than a hair. Your next brain-boggling challenge was to create a whole human body consisting of 300 different types of cell and guaranteed to last a lifetime. And you had just nine months to do it in.

HOW YOU BECAME YOU

You started off as a single cell, but within 30 hours you divided into two cells and you kept on dividing. In fact your cells haven't stopped splitting to this day.

In your first few days of existence you drifted lazily down the fallopian tube to the uterus. There, you and your mum created a life-support machine called a placenta. The placenta was the ultimate free lunch – it was connected to you by a feeding tube called the umbilical cord. You got all the oxygen and food a growing baby needed even if your poor mum was starving. Unborn babies don't talk to their mums but if they did they might say things like this…

22 days

Hey, Mum, can you hear me? My heart is beating! Pity I haven't got a head yet but I'm working on it!

38 days

At last I've got a head and a nose, but I haven't got fingers and toes yet and I'm smaller than a grape. Hmm – time to do some growing – hey, Mum, I'm starving – got any pizza?

Week 7

Well, Mum, that's my liver and kidneys working. I'm feeling a bit more human every day! Now all I need is some food and drink to process – hint, hint!

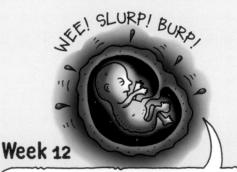

Week 12

It's great relaxing in this fluid bag – it's like a private swimming pool and I can drink as much as I like and do somersaults. OH NO – I'm weeing. Oh well, I'll just drink it again – slurp, burp!

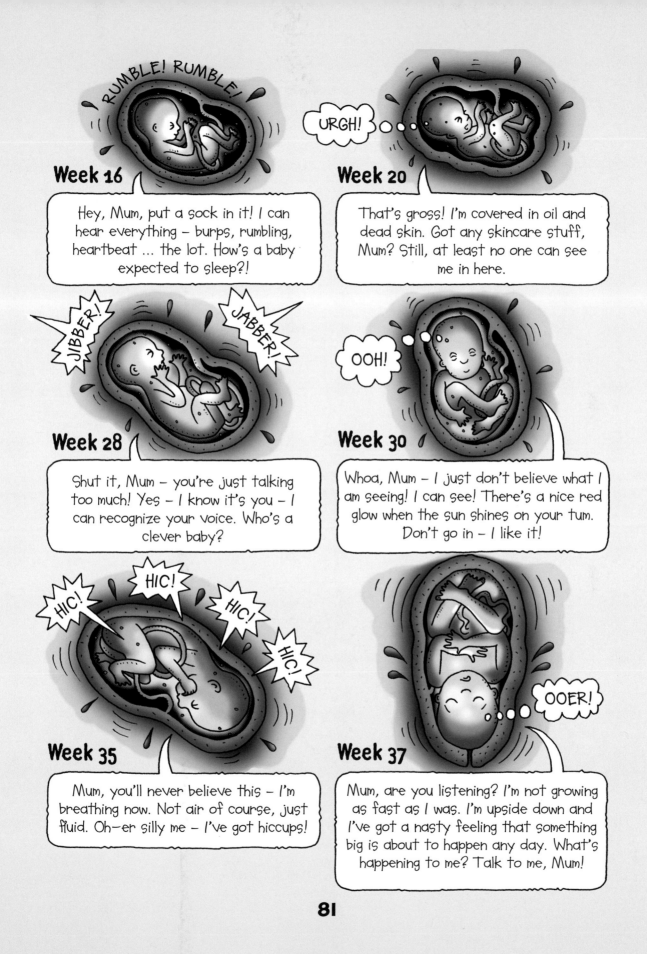

HOW TO BE A BORN WINNER

Your unborn life was one long holiday. You were warm and comfy and everything was laid on – food, drink, central heating and entertainment. You might have felt a bit bored just hanging around, but fortunately you didn't know what bored meant.

Then one day it changed. No one asked you, no one warned you. All at once you were fighting for your life. It was the most danger you have ever known. You were being born. I don't expect you remember it – so here's what happened.

There you were, happily hanging out. Suddenly the fluid bag bursts and the sides of the uterus start squeezing. In the next few hours you had to corkscrew your head out into the world while it was being crushed out of shape. (Fortunately your skull bones hadn't yet joined together or you would have a very strangely shaped head today.) This was scary – your first few seconds were life or death.

Once you were born you had seconds to fill your lungs with air and rearrange your heart blood vessels in a way that would kill an adult. If you failed, you might have died, but you didn't – you made it! Welcome to the world! No wonder you were bawling your little head off!

SNIP!

GOO GOO!

Once you were born you needed help. First of all you needed to get rid of your feeding tube. A midwife or doctor would have clamped it in two places and cut through it (don't worry, it didn't hurt). Luckily the cut end of the tube dropped off later and now you've got a cheesy souvenir of your first birthday – a belly button.

Next you needed to be cleaned up and kept warm. Being born is like getting chucked in a freezing swimming pool. Fortunately you had special fat that actually produced heat to make a bit of warmth.

When you were born you were useless at everything. The thing was, your brain wasn't ready – it simply couldn't handle walking, talking or co-ordination. But if your head had grown much bigger it couldn't have got out of your mum. So instead your boggled baby brain went into overdrive to catch up…

Bet you never knew!

Weird things happened to you while you were inside your mum. At various stages you had gills like fish breathe through (except yours didn't work) three pairs of kidneys, webbed fingers and toes and a hairy body. Luckily all these things sorted themselves out before you were born.

 Within a year your brain increased in size 2.5 times and 60 per cent of your food went to supply it.

 By the time you were two you were able to tell your mum when your nappy needed changing.

By the time you were three you could help tidy your room (although some kids never quite reach this stage).

By the time you were four you had the same level of brain activity as your parents – although I bet you couldn't read this book.

Now that's progress!

BOUNCING BABIES

The story so far… The twins are bored of being bored teenagers, so they ask Junior to change them back to their proper age. But with Junior in charge, disaster is just around the corner…

I'VE GONE A BIT TOO FAR!

ICKLE GOO-GOO DWIBBLE!*

WAAAAAGH!**

OH NO – HAVE I GOT TO CHANGE NAPPIES AGAIN?

THIS TAKES ME BACK!

*THIS IS S-O-O SCARY! EVERYTHING IS UPSIDE DOWN AND I CAN'T BREATHE THROUGH MY MOUTH!
**THIS IS SO EMBARRASSING I CAN'T STOP DRIBBLING AND MY NAPPY IS ABOUT TO EXPLODE!

The difficulties seeing and breathing were normal. As a newborn baby you saw the world upside down because your brain hadn't worked out how to turn the signals from your retinas the right way up. Not being able to breathe through your mouth helped you to feed and breathe at the same time.

But there was a long list of things you couldn't do…

List of things I CAN'T do

1 Walk - I can't balance or coordinate my body.

2 Eat proper food. Boring!

3 Control when I pee or poo. Well, who cares, that's what nappies were invented for!

Hmmm… lovely and warm!

4 Talk - my voice box is in the wrong place. And even if I could talk I don't know any words…..

5 Play football.

6 Do science homework.

7 Just about anything else.

8 Hmm - maybe it's easier to make a list of what I CAN do?

It's not much of a list but that doesn't matter. After all, when you were a baby you had grown-ups to look after you. What's more you had sneaky ways to control them, such as…

- Large eyes and a cute round face. Human brains are wired up to find baby faces cute and they even go gooey over other creatures with large eyes and round faces – like kittens.
- When babies cry their mum's heartbeat speeds up. Crying also switches on mum's milk supply.

Meanwhile the Normal parents are getting frazzled by their baby children…

And just when you think things can't go any more horribly wrong. They do…

WEARY WRINKLIES

In a horrible explosion of light the machine malfunctions big time. This time the ageing process has gone way, way too far...

If you dared to ask your grandparents or possibly your more wrinkly teachers about growing old, they would probably agree that ageing feels like a cruel trick played by our bodies. In fact, growing old is proof that the old saying "what can go wrong will go wrong" is true for the human body. But why?

Well, it's due to damage outside and inside. On the one hand any body that's been around for a time collects damage that it can't repair. There are scars and missing teeth. And then there's the effect of ultraviolet light from the sun. These invisible rays give you sunburn if you stay in the sun too long and they slowly age the skin. Meanwhile, things are going wonky inside the cells.

Although everyone is very upset at the accident, the other shrinking scientists can't resist the temptation to investigate the ageing cells in the boy's hairy, saggy ears.

Remember how your mitochondria make energy using glucose and oxygen? Well, the process releases oxygen atoms known as free radicals

The free radicals can damage your DNA

Enzymes try to repair the damage

ENERGY! ENERGY! ENERGY! ENERGY!

Ageing body cell

Substances called antioxidants (these include vitamins C and E) mop up free radicals

WOBBLE! SHAKE!

MAKE ME YOUNG, YOU YOUNG WHIPPER-SNAPPERS!

THIS CELL IS ON ITS LAST LEGS – IF IT HAD LEGS.

IT'S CERTAINLY PAST ITS CELL–BY DATE.

HAS ANYONE SEEN MY GLASSES?

Every second of the day your cells are under attack from oxygen, the very stuff they need to stay alive. What's more, just by doing what they do they damage themselves. Of course your cells try to put things right – but eventually they fail and die off.

It's not exactly the end of the world for your body. After all, your cells die off all the time and other cells divide to make more cells. The problem is that there's a limit to this process. Let's take a closer look at these sickly cells.

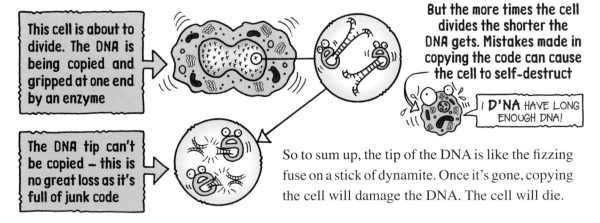

This cell is about to divide. The DNA is being copied and gripped at one end by an enzyme

The DNA tip can't be copied – this is no great loss as it's full of junk code

But the more times the cell divides the shorter the DNA gets. Mistakes made in copying the code can cause the cell to self-destruct

I D'NA HAVE LONG ENOUGH DNA!

So to sum up, the tip of the DNA is like the fizzing fuse on a stick of dynamite. Once it's gone, copying the cell will damage the DNA. The cell will die.

AWFUL AGEING

As the years go by and cells die off, the signs of ageing on the poor old body become painfully obvious. They're certainly obvious on the twins and Junior...

Each hair turns white because the cells that make colour die off. The more white hairs you have the greyer your hair looks

Oddly enough black eyelashes don't go white

Hair is thinning due to loss of hair-producing cells

Male eyebrows get bushier

The ears and nose look bigger because these bits grow throughout life

Hearing lost as sound-sensitive fibres in the cochlea die off

Male ear and nostril hair starts to sprout

EVERY JOINT IN MY BODY ACHES!

Lens thickens in the eyeball making it harder for the eyeball to focus. This also cuts down on the light reaching the retina

THANKS – TWO SUGARS, PLEASE!

THEY'RE AS WRINKLY AS A CABBAGE BUT NOT AS TASTY.

Sense of smell weakens as sensor cells die off in the nose. More than half of the over-eighties lose the sense of smell. At least the twins are spared the stomach-turning stink of Junior's trainers (he hasn't taken them off for 84 years)

Damage by ultraviolet light reduces skin collagen and elastin – the proteins that make your skin springy. The skin gets thinner and saggy. Skin creases into lines (it takes 200,000 frowns to make a line so don't start now)

As people grow older and weaker they exercise less, which weakens them further. Meanwhile fat can build up in their arteries – the vital plumbing that takes blood to crucial body bits such as the heart and brain. Blockages can cause a heart attack or stroke when part of the brain dies. Worse still, a build-up of DNA copying mistakes can sometimes create a rebel cell – a cell that doesn't do the decent thing and die when its time is up. Instead it divides out of control. It's become a cancer cell. Cancer cells can spread to other parts of the body with fatal results. Ultimately the poor old body can't carry on. It's a brain-boggling living machine guaranteed to last a lifetime – but even the best-designed machine will break down one day.

GOLDEN GRANNIES (AND GRANDPAS)

So far this chapter has been about as much fun as cutting grandpa's toenails. So does that mean that life for older people is sad and sour? You might not agree but I think there's a good side to getting on a bit. If you don't believe me ask any older person. In fact, let's ask Albert Crumble – the world's oldest teacher...

The Horrible Science Interview with Albert Crumble

HS: IS THERE A BETTER SIDE TO GETTING ON A BIT?

ALBERT: OH YES, I'M 101 YEARS OLD BUT STILL GOING STRONG. AND I RECKON I'M A BETTER TEACHER NOW BECAUSE I'M MORE TOLERANT OF THE CHILDREN'S MISTAKES.

HS: DOES EXPERIENCE HELP?

ALBERT: OH YES – I CAN SEE THE BIGGER PICTURE AND NOT GET BOGGED DOWN IN DETAILS. MY WORD-POWER IS BETTER AND I KNOW WHAT'S IMPORTANT IN LIFE – PEOPLE AND GOOD HEALTH. OH, YES WHO NEEDS YOUTH?

HS: WHAT DO YOUR PUPILS THINK?

ALBERT: OH THEY THINK I'M GREAT EXCEPT WHEN I WHACK THEM WITH MY CANE. PITY I'M NOT SO STRONG AS I USED TO BE...

HS: SO YOU'RE NOT A CLAPPED-OUT OVER-THE-HILL OLD HAS-BEEN?

GRR – COME BACK HERE! I'LL TAN YOUR SCRAWNY HIDE!

OK, so I made up Albert but I do have some genuine good news. These days more and more older people are having artificial bits called implants installed inside their bodies to keep them going longer. They include nice new replacement joints and heart pacemakers to keep the old ticker ticking with a regular rhythm.

Meanwhile, scientists have come up with a whole list of things that people can do to slow down the ageing process. These really do work – so let's imagine we brought them together in a special school for senior citizens…

Bet you never knew!

In 1976, a Greek runner named Dimitrion Yordanidis ran a marathon in Athens. A marathon is a gruelling muscle-wrenching 42-km run but it was worse for dogged Dimitrion than for most people. He was 98 years old at the time.

RUN, DAD, RUN!

KEEP GOING, GRANDAD!

GO FOR IT, GREAT GRANDAD!

PUFF!

WHEEZE!

HOORAY FOR GREAT, GREAT GRANDAD!

Granny and Grandpa getting on a bit?

BUMBLE!

FUMBLE!

MUMBLE!

GRUMBLE!

FUMBLE!

BUMBLE!

Send them to the Horrible Science Senior Citizen School!

New healthy canteen - fresh fruit and lots of green vegetables rich in Vitamin C and antioxidants to keep them young (or at least stop them getting more wrinkly).

Sport isn't just for the young 'uns! Daily exercise sessions in the gym to strengthen those rickety old hearts, bones and muscles.

Lots of books, plus brainteasers, jigsaw puzzles and logic games to keep the old grey matter sparking.

FANCY A GAME OF CHESS?

SURE! AFTER I'VE HAD A JOG AND EATEN MY BROCCOLI SOUP!

So what about the ancient children in the Normal house? Are they ready for long-distance running or senior citizen school?

NO WAY! JUST TURN ME BACK INTO A KID OR I'LL BRAIN YOU WITH MY WALKING STICK!

AND I'LL SHOVE MY EXTRA-STRONG PEPPERMINTS UP YOUR NOSTRILS!

Oh dear, the B.A.D. machine is broken. Does that mean that the children and Junior are destined for an old folks' home? Is this book about to have an unhappy ending?

THE WONDER OF YOU!

As a result of an accident the children of the Normal family have been artificially aged. It looks like their next birthday cake will have so many candles it'll be a major fire hazard. But just then Mr Fluffy comes bounding to the rescue with a spare B.A.D. unit from the lab.

So what have the Normal family learned from their experiences with the shrinking scientists?

Hmm – I couldn't have put it better. The body really is amazing! I mean, just imagine Junior's body could speak for itself – what would it say?

Doesn't Junior's body sound like a boring Dr Grimgrave-style doctor? Well, that's because it wants to keep him fit and healthy. And that's all your body wants for you too.

Your body has always been there for you. Before you were even born it built itself cell by cell using the genes that your parents gave you. Ever since it's kept you breathing, walking, talking, eating, digesting, learning and exploring your world. Without a body you'd be dead as a dinosaur. With its help you can make your dreams come true. Now that really is brain-boggling!

SPOT THE HORRIBLE BODY BITS QUIZ

Here are a selection of horrible bits and pieces from this book...

How to play...

You will need a piece of paper and pencil to keep your score.

You get ONE point for saying what each horrible item is.

ONE point for remembering what chapter they came from (without peeking)

And ONE point for being able to find them by looking back in this book.

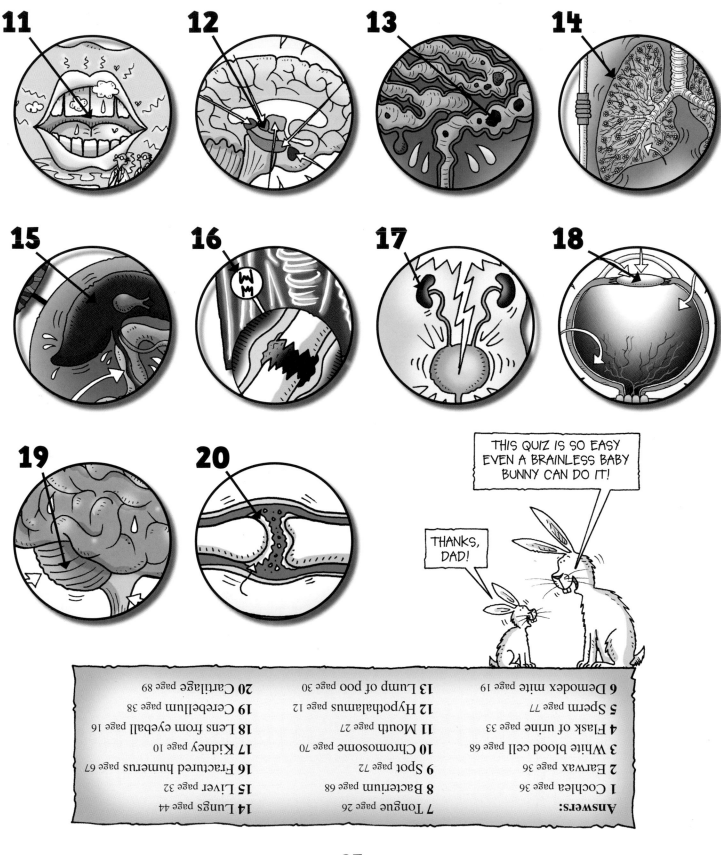

BRAIN-BOGGLING INDEX